Negative Thoughts Happen

How To Find Your Inner Ally When Your Inner Critic Shows Up

Diana M. Garcia, LMHC

16pt

Copyright Page from the Original Book

Publisher's Note

This publication is designed to provide accurate and authoritative information in regard to the subject matter covered. It is sold with the understanding that the publisher is not engaged in rendering psychological, financial, legal, or other professional services. If expert assistance or counseling is needed, the services of a competent professional should be sought.

NEW HARBINGER PUBLICATIONS is a registered trademark of New Harbinger Publications, Inc.

New Harbinger Publications is an employee-owned company.

Copyright © 2023 by Diana M. Garcia
                    New Harbinger Publications, Inc.
                    5720 Shattuck Avenue
                    Oakland, CA 94609
                    www.newharbinger.com

All Rights Reserved

Interior Design by Michele Waters-Kermes;
Acquired by Elizabeth Hollis Hansen; Edited by Kristi Hein

Library of Congress Cataloging-in-Publication Data on file

TABLE OF CONTENTS

Introduction	v
PART 1: The Inner Critic	1
Chapter 1: What Is Negative Self-Talk?	1
Chapter 2: Why Is Negative Self-Talk So Common?	5
Chapter 3: Why Is Your Mind Such a Buzzkill?	10
Chapter 4: Language Doesn't Always Have Your Back	15
Chapter 5: When Is the Inner Critic Born?	21
Chapter 6: Your Inner Critic Is Not Living Rent-Free in Your Head	29
Chapter 7: Relationship with Self	34
Chapter 8: Relationship with Others	39
Chapter 9: Relationship with Achievements	43
Chapter 10: Your Inner Critic Has Its Moments	47
Chapter 11: You've Tried It All, with No Success	52
PART 2: How to Find Your Inner Ally	58
Chapter 12: Creating Distance from Your Thoughts	61
Chapter 13: Your Mind, Making Sense of Who You Are	66
Chapter 14: Opening to Your Experiences	80
Chapter 15: Is That a Shark?	85
Chapter 16: Coming Back to the Now	93
Chapter 17: But My Mind Doesn't Stay Quiet	102
Chapter 18: Treating Yourself Like a Loving Friend	111
Chapter 19: Wait—Who's Noticing?	119
Chapter 20: Keep Raising Your Right Hand	128
Chapter 21: Seeking Your Inner Compass	135
Chapter 22: Calibrating Your Compass	141
Chapter 23: Shining a Light	149
Chapter 24: Showing Up	156
Chapter 25: Moving Forward	165
Conclusion	175
Acknowledgments	179
References	180
Back Cover Material	188

TABLE OF CONTENT

Introduction v

PART 1: The Inner Critic 1

Chapter 1: Who is Your Inner Critic? 1
Chapter 2: Why Is Negative Self-Talk So Common? 5
Chapter 3: Write Your Mind Such a Bazaar 10
Chapter 4: Language Doesn't Always Have Your Back ... 16
Chapter 5: When is the Inner Critic Born? 21
Chapter 6: Your Inner Critic Is Not Living Rent-Free in Your Head ... 29
Chapter 7: Relationship with Self 34
Chapter 8: Relationship with Others 39
Chapter 9: Relationship with Achievements 43
Chapter 10: Your Inner Critic Has Its Moment 47
Chapter 11: You're Not Alone with Insecurity 52

PART 2: How to Find Your Inner Ally 53

Chapter 12: Creating Distance from Your Thoughts 61
Chapter 13: Mindful Making Sense of Who You Are 66
Chapter 14: Opening to Your Experiences 69
Chapter 15: Is That a Shift? 86
Chapter 16: Coming Back to the Now 93
Chapter 17: Bug in My Mind Doesn't Say Critic 102
Chapter 18: Treating Yourself Like a Loving Friend .. 111
Chapter 19: Vale—What Noticing 119
Chapter 20: Keep Sitting Your Right Hand 125
Chapter 21: Seeking Your Inner Compass 135
Chapter 22: Calibrating Your Compass 141
Chapter 23: Shining a Light 149
Chapter 24: Showing Up 157
Chapter 25: Moving Forward 165
Conclusion 175
Acknowledgments 179
References 180
Back Cover Material 188

"If you have ever experienced negative self-talk (and I bet you have!), then this is the book you've been waiting for. With empathy and wisdom, it reassures you that there's nothing wrong with you, and offers tangible tools to break free from the grip of your inner critic. Prepare to embark on a transformative journey toward a life filled with self-compassion and the fulfillment of your dreams."

—**Rikke Kjelgaard,** psychologist, author, acceptance and commitment therapy (ACT) trainer, and chief "rock'n'roller" at www.rikkekjelgaard.com

"An invaluable resource for those seeking to live a more meaningful life by changing the relationship you have with the negative thoughts residing in your head, aka your 'inner critic!' As a psychology professor and psychotherapist, I highly recommend this empowering book. Through insightful guidance and effective strategies from ACT, it equips readers with practical tools—increasing awareness, flexibility, and values-driven behavior that leads to a rich, meaningful life."

—**Lisa Arango,** psychology professor at Florida International University, psychotherapist for more than twenty years, and creator of the Happy Marriage Formula

"Negative thoughts are a universal experience for every person on the planet, and it's a natural part of being human. However, our self-criticism can hinder us from living the life we desire. If you're looking for ways to cope with your inner critic, I highly recommend this book. It provides practical and engaging tips, strategies, and exercises to help you strengthen your inner ally."

—**Joe Oliver,** coauthor of *The Mindfulness and Acceptance Workbook for Self Esteem,* and founder of Contextual Consulting

"A must-read for human beings! *Negative Thoughts Happen* is a simple, straightforward guide to changing your relationship with negative thoughts. Filled with engaging and powerful exercises, it offers genuinely helpful guidance aimed at helping you build new relationships with your thoughts. Negative thoughts can feel like a burden to bear, but Diana Garcia's relatable, conversational tone offers real hope for lightening that burden."

—**Miranda Morris, PhD,** clinical psychologist, peer-reviewed ACT trainer, cofounder of True North Therapy and Training, and past president of the Association for Contextual Behavioral Science

"There is not a human alive who has failed to be tormented at times by their inner critic. This kind and gentle book walks into the persistent self-doubt many of us grapple with and shows how the inner critic works, while offering transformative insights and tools grounded in ACT for finding an inner ally that will change your relationship to the negative thoughts that hound you. For anyone feeling ensnared by negative self-talk and seeking meaningful, brave living, this book is a must-read. Dive in, reflect, and experiment. These pages contain a path to a life well-lived, beyond the confines of that inner bully."

—**Steven C. Hayes, PhD,** Nevada Foundation Professor in the department of psychology at the University of Nevada, Reno; and co-originator of ACT

To my mother, for always being my unwavering ally.

Introduction

You're so stupid.

You're such a loser.

No one will ever love you.

You're too much! No one will ever put up with you.

You're so incompetent! How could you ever have believed you'd get that job?

Of course you got ghosted—have you looked in the mirror lately?

You're so cold. Do you even have a heartbeat?

You're so worthless—you can't even get your kids to school on time.

And on and on goes the list of negative trash your brain tells you. These are common phrases I hear on repeat from therapy clients. Because negative self-talk happens constantly, our minds are programmed for it. I have my own version (yes, therapists are not golden unicorns immune to the workings of the human mind).

For many of us, our negative self-talk is so relentless that it's developed into a constant inner critic.

And that's the premise of this book. But not the entire premise. This book will provide knowledge and skills to help you change your relationship with this inner critic and live a brave life.

Because guess what? You deserve to live a meaningful life, no matter what that internal bully says about you. You deserve to be able to look back when you're eighty with a drink in your hand, grays in your hair, and a smile on your face, knowing that you've lived a worthwhile life.

But let's keep it real (because that's my promise throughout): It's not all rainbows and butterflies. To get there, you must be willing to release the inner critic's hold, be ready to feel uncomfortable, and accept that you will sometimes fail. Life can throw you curveballs at every unexpected turn.

The name of the game here is *psychological flexibility*. Psychological flexibility is being present with your thoughts and feelings and still acting on your values. It's a fancy way of saying being able to adapt to life's curveballs and your internal baggage. Imagine being the world champion at *Twister* in the game of life:
- Left foot, green = Your mom left when you were twelve (external)

- Right hand, red = You feel loved and appreciated by close friends (internal)
- Left hand, yellow = You have unexpected, intense panic attacks (internal)
- Right foot, blue = You find the person who makes your heart flutter (external)
- Left foot, red = You feel like a fraud and an imposter at your dream job (internal)
- Right hand, blue = Your beautiful, healthy baby girl is born (external)

Winning this game of life means being able to remain flexible while playing; to not get bogged down by trying to avoid or struggle with the unavoidable. Because there's no way around it: Things have been tough and will keep being tough. Despite what our culture often tells us—that we should *always* feel good and stay positive. That's tough (if not nearly impossible) to do when you're playing the game of life and when your inner world doesn't have the same rules.

In part 2 of this book, I'll provide tools to increase your flexibility using a proven method called acceptance and commitment therapy (ACT). ACT is a model of psychotherapy that offers interventions and tools to help you be more present in your life, tune in to your values as a never-ending guide, and learn strategies to help you engage with the painful thoughts, feelings, urges, physical sensations, or memories that tend to get in the way.

How to Use This Book

Before you jump into the book, here are some loose guidelines:

- Use a journal, notes app, or Google Docs to do the exercises and self-reflect. To gain the most from the activities, keep it all in the same place. Ideally, you'll be able to return to it when you get stuck.
- Take the time to do the reflection exercises. I know, I know—who has the time? It's easy to skip the activities and keep reading, but I recommend engaging in each exercise as you first encounter it.
- Go easy on yourself while gaining new insights, learning new skills, and trying to behave differently. Being an imperfect human is part of the bargain. Give yourself grace and kindness as you go through this book (and ultimately, through life).

PART I

The Inner Critic

Chapter 1

What Is Negative Self-Talk?

Self-talk is all the thoughts your mind makes up about you. Imagine you had an ever-present roommate giving you unsolicited feedback on every aspect of yourself, including your worth, appearance, and choices. This can happen entirely in your head (between you and your constant roommate), or you might say it aloud—in conversations with others or yourself—or write it down in a journal.

If this roommate is not so pleasant—if most of what they say to you is negative, questioning, or critical—then you're dealing with *negative* self-talk.

In popular culture, the antidote to negative self-talk is to practice positive self-talk. This means having more endearing thoughts about yourself and trying hard to believe them. When you first picked up this book, you might have thought, *Oh no! Not another book telling me to practice positive affirmations.* Don't worry; this is not that type of book. (Although if that works for you, keep on keeping on.) The goal here is all about doing what works to bring you closer to a valued life.

But there's nothing wrong with you if you've tried to embrace all the positive affirmations with little to no long-term success. Nothing is fatally wrong with you; this just means you have a human brain wired to protect you. It treats emotional threats—like a failure, or others' judgment—the same as physical threats. Our minds tend to direct more time and attention to negative thoughts.

Now think about how much time you spend thinking about yourself. At some point, some of those thoughts are bound to be negative. Your negative self-talk serves specific purposes—such as trying to keep you from making a mistake at work or getting hurt in a relationship. You can see why having an inner critic is common and can become problematic.

Negative self-talk is a component of many mental health disorders, including depression, anxiety, trauma, eating disorders, body dysmorphia, and personality disorders, to name a few. In 2019, nearly fifty million American adults experienced a mental illness (Reinert, Fritze, and Nguyen 2021). Add in the COVID-19 pandemic's impact on our mental health. According to the World Health Organization

(2022), the global prevalence of anxiety and depression increased by 25 percent during the first year of the pandemic.

Sit with those numbers—and negative self-talk's impact on our population. And the percentage of those of us who struggle with negative thoughts is not limited to those with diagnosable disorders. When life becomes difficult, it makes sense to have some negative thoughts. And eventually, those negative thoughts might focus on self-judgment.

Considering the pandemic, it makes complete sense that at some point you've had negative thoughts about the state of the world. Probably more so when you kept furiously checking the news. It also makes sense if you felt scared, powerless, and uncertain. You might have even started to judge yourself: *You should be more resilient, You should be handling this better, Put on a brave face for your kids,* and so on, even though it's normal to have a distressing reaction to a painful, frightening event.

But your mind still finds ways to judge you harshly. Isn't that curious? Your mind judges you when you're in pain. I saw this often during the pandemic with many of my clients. Even though they reacted normally to a stressful situation, their inner critic would somehow turn the spotlight on them.

Now, the pandemic is just one negative situation (granted, on a massive scale unprecedented in our lifetimes), yet life has this curious way of being unpredictable. And when you experience a bump in the road, one reaction could be negative self-talk.

As you can see, negative self-talk can be a ubiquitous experience. It's one way we respond to and attempt to cope with life's difficulties. In the next chapter, we'll dive into the features of the human brain and mind that'll help you better understand why this happens.

Chapter 2

Why Is Negative Self-Talk So Common?

Our brains are wired to be problem-solving machines, constantly looking for solutions. And to some degree, that's fantastic—it's one of our superpowers as a species. It's helped us not only survive but achieve tremendous things. Our brain's ability to solve complex problems has allowed us to build cities, create the Eiffel Tower, and establish the World Wide Web. We can thank the brains of individuals working alone or together for these things.

This also reveals a straightforward and effective formula in the outside world: When you're presented with a problem, find a solution.

Problem: You keep ordering delivery and spending a fortune.

Solution: Subscribe to a meal box service and start cooking.

That's a straightforward problem; let's consider a more nuanced situation.

Problem: You and your partner keep arguing over minor stuff, like who's supposed to start the laundry.

In this instance, your problem-solving mind might give you a few options:

Potential solution: Keep yelling at your partner, expecting them to get it eventually. (Although you've tried this with no success. How weird, that yelling at your partner isn't getting the message across.)

Potential solution: Try to hear and understand each other's side, truly. It's not really about the laundry. Be vulnerable and express how you feel.

Potential solution: Do it yourself to prevent future fights over this. Surely you won't get resentful.

Potential solution: Break up over the continued arguments; doing your laundry is much easier.

See how skilled your mind is at drafting a menu of options to explore? One of these solutions might work. And if it doesn't work, your mind will return to the drawing board and adjust, based on the new data.

Your mind is trained to hold on to this golden formula because it works well in the outside world. And your mind naturally applies this formula to your inner world. When I say inner world, I mean your thoughts, feelings, physical sensations, and memories.

Your mind activates its problem-solving abilities when it perceives an inner-world experience as a problem. And—news flash—your mind perceives anything negative or uncomfortable as an issue. Your mind considers the following as problems to solve:

Feeling: Fear

Mind: *Something must be wrong; turn off this sensation or avoid it at all costs!*

Thoughts: *I'm such a fraud at work; they will eventually figure it out.*

Mind: *I cannot let others find this out. Work harder, take on more, and don't speak up, to prevent others from seeing it too.*

Physical sensation: *My heart is beating faster. I'm sweating and flushed.*

Mind: *Uh-oh, danger! Something is wrong. Maybe I'm having a heart attack. I have been eating like crap lately. Can't remember when I last did cardio. Oh no. This. Is. The. End!*

Memory: *Remember that time in middle school when I became painfully aware of how awkward I was? That group of kids kept giving me weird looks and making snide comments.*

Mind: *Don't think about that! What's wrong with me for going there?! I should be so past that; it was years ago. Shut that part down! So what if I was awkward? Look how well put together I am now! Right?*

The minute your mind identifies something in your inner world as a threat, it immediately goes to work, helping you "deal" with it. You distract yourself, overcompensate, avoid the things that make you feel bad, or obsessively stew, because at least that feels like doing something.

You must commend your mind's effort, although this book would be unnecessary if your mind had it all figured out, if it could solve the problem of self-talk in a way that helped you overcome it. Because then your mind would have solved all these complex inner-world problems like a champ.

But there's a fatal flaw here. This golden formula does not work for our inner world. Don't take my word for it. Stop and consider: Have all your mind's potential solutions worked to get rid of your painful inner experiences—that uncomfortable thought that you don't belong, or that cringy feeling of rejection?

You might think, *When I distract myself by binge-watching all five seasons of my favorite show, it temporarily works and takes away the uncomfortable experiences.* And it's true: Distraction is a strategy that can seem to work in the short term. But once you turn off the TV, you're plagued with those same thoughts and feelings you desperately tried to avoid.

So again, have all your mind's potential solutions worked to eliminate your stuff in the long run? Have you found the magical solution to turn off all these negative thoughts and shut up your inner critic forever? The answer's probably no.

I know I've frantically tried to do everything my mind tells me to do to eliminate my negative thoughts. I even became a therapist, and maybe some small part of me hoped that would help me figure it all out. Then I'd stop doubting myself, silence my inner critic, and stop feeling "less." Wasn't that part of the buy-in?

I learned the hard way that's not how it works. I still deal with my stuff and hear my inner critic comment on my life, particularly the important matters.

How meta is it that even as I'm writing a book on the inner critic, it causes my inner critic to get louder? But I know that's just how brains are programmed. And I also know my problem-solving mind wouldn't be so loud if my actions didn't matter.

Ultimately, my inner critic reminds me of what's important to me. I can hear it and think, *Well, writing this book is important to me. And it's a value of mine to be courageous despite what my inner critic says.*

This isn't to say the inner critic or the mind is always worth listening to. Especially since it often says *you* are at fault for not listening to *it* well enough. It cannot grasp that maybe the formula is the problem here. And there are some excellent reasons for that.

Exercise

List all the inner experiences your mind tries to convince you are problems to solve or eliminate. Include recurring thoughts, feelings, physical sensations, and memories.

Chapter 3
Why Is Your Mind Such a Buzzkill?

Believe it or not, the fact that our minds are primed for negativity is a strength, in a way. For one, it has literally kept us alive. From an evolutionary perspective, our ancestors had to constantly be on the lookout for life-threatening dangers. This constant tendency to scan our environment for potential threats and focus on what could be harmful has been reinforced over time. This pattern influenced how our minds evolved.

Imagine two prehistoric men, Jim and Fred, living close to nature. Jim is the more anxious of the two, constantly worrying about potential dangers and playing it safe. In comparison, Fred is more laid-back and chill. He reacts to threats when directly confronting them but takes a more lackadaisical approach.

They both step outside their huts every morning and gaze into the wild. Both decide whether today is a good day to go on the prowl and stock up on food. They both see a blurry figure on the horizon that's hard to distinguish. Jim assumes it's a big scary saber-toothed cat waiting to attack, whereas Fred assumes it's a bush.

The thing is, 99 percent of the time, Fred is correct. So he leaves his hut and hunts for dinner. And 99 percent of the time, he returns victorious and can feed his family. Despite the evidence to the contrary—like Fred going out and returning—Jim still assesses that blurry figure as a potential threat. Some days, the family eats berries and roots collected by his mate, and some days they go a little hungry.

You might be thinking, *Jim, get with the program!* But recall that 1 percent of the time, Jim is correct in his assessment.

One day they both step outside and make the same assumptions. Fred goes on his merry way again, and Jim begrudgingly joins the gatherers. On his hunt, Fred is attacked by a saber-tooth and never seen again.

Kelly G. Wilson, one of the creators of ACT, says, "We're capable of missing lunch many, many times, but we can only be lunch once (and after that, maybe dinner and breakfast, but that's largely up to the bear)" (2010).

Although many of you don't need to constantly look for danger around every corner, your mind doesn't know that and continues to be on the lookout. Your mind would rather assume something is a threat and potentially get it wrong than risk ending up like Fred.

As for that anxious fellow Jim, he went on to live many more days and passed on his anxious genes. We have all the Jims to thank for keeping our species—and our propensity for negativity—alive. This reinforced the development of our negativity bias, which also powers negative self-talk.

According to neuroscience, negativity bias is the brain's propensity to look out for, recall, and hold on to adverse events more strongly. That's why you might:
- More quickly recall instances of being criticized
- More strongly, and perhaps more quickly, react to adverse events/situations
- Focus more on negative thoughts, including negative self-talk
- Recall painful or traumatic memories more strongly than more benign or pleasant ones
- Be inclined to scan your environment for potential threats even when things are well

Neuroscientist Rick Hanson once said, "Your brain is like Velcro for negative experiences but Teflon for positive ones" (2013). Special circuits in your brain encode negative experiences to memory much more quickly than positive ones. It takes your brain more work to hold on to positive experiences, whereas the negative ones stick easily.

This negative bias develops early on. Since you were young, your brain—including your inner critic—has been focusing on and reacting robustly to negativity. Your inner critic has gotten more stage time because it falls within this negativity bias category. And weirdly, focusing on your negative qualities is part of your mind's way of trying to keep you safe.

Another vital factor is the role played by being part of the group. Back to Fred and Jim for a second: They were part of a larger tribe. They were the designated hunters, but different members focused on building huts, cooking, or raising the little ones. You see, back then, being part of a group was essential to increase your odds of survival.

If you got kicked out of the group, you would most likely die alone. This old part of your brain, wired for connection, is part of the reason that it can feel so excruciatingly painful when you get excluded or rejected from the group. An old part of your brain still links this to potential death.

Sometimes our negative thoughts include things like *She must hate me* or *I'm such a weirdo; I don't understand social cues*. When negative, self-critical thoughts contain something that can lead to exclusion, your mind might focus on it—to fix it or hide it to prevent rejection. But as you'll see, that doesn't make listening to these negative thoughts worth your while.

Say you're checking Instagram and see your good friend Phoebe's posts about her sick cat. You think, *I can't believe it's been so long since I've checked in with her. I'm such a jackass. We used to be so close—I should've known about this!*

How might you respond to your self-critical thought?

One way would be to withdraw and shut down. Another could be to self-evaluate, then address the lack of connection you're feeling by checking about her cat. If you take the second option, your self-critical thoughts have helped you. You've demonstrated the psychological flexibility necessary to use that thought to act on what you value.

I find that individuals who struggle with a sharp inner critic tend to lean toward the first response. They let their inner critic convince them to withdraw because they believe its scolding judgment.

Exercise

- Reflect on what it means that since childhood your brain has been programmed to give the inner critic more airtime.
- Imagine what might happen if you did something radically different the next time your inner critic says something about you. What if you weren't stuck doing what your brain might be wired to make you do?

Chapter 4

Language Doesn't Always Have Your Back

Now you understand how the deck is stacked against you from an evolutionary perspective. And that's not all. There's something you should know about language and learning.

When we're learning a language, we make two-way associations. For instance, if you show your toddler a mango and repeat the word "mango," the toddler will associate that object with the word "mango." If you then ask your toddler, "Where's the mango?" they can point to it. They've made the following two associations (Hayes and Smith 2005):

Object Mango → Word Mango

Word Mango → Object Mango

To get your kid to try the mango, you teach them that it's yummy by making the sound "yummm." You ask them, "What is yummm?" They point at the mango, and now more associations are going on:

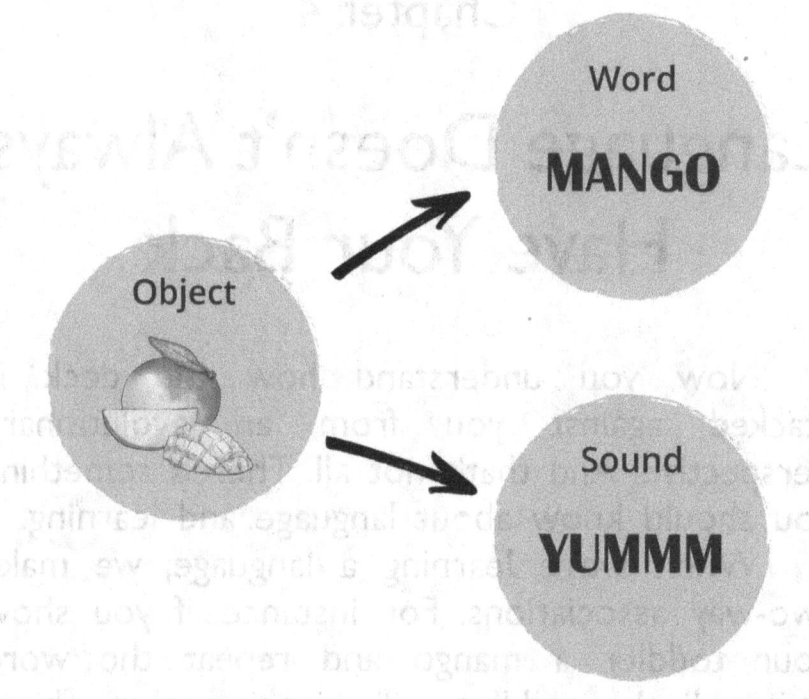

Your toddler will eventually become able to make the association between the sound "yummm" and the word "mango," even though you didn't directly teach them that the word "mango" is associated with "yummm."

This might seem like a no-brainer, yet this ability to make these associations separates us from the rest of mammals. Human toddlers make these associations without much thought, whereas you'd have to actively train any nonhuman animal to make them.

Another cool thing is the ability to learn from others' experiences. If your friend tells you to steer clear of that new sushi spot because they got sick, you can learn from their experience. In essence, you can try to spare yourself both a miserable illness and your inner critic's beating up on you for foolishly patronizing that sushi place.

This ability to make these complex connections has some clear advantages for our species. It has allowed us to surpass, in some ways, all other species on this planet, even though we're not the fastest or strongest, nor can we shoot spider silk out of our hands. It's also another reason we strongly rely on being part of a social group. This allowed us to not have to learn solely from our brainpower but to pool our collective brainpower to learn and advance as a species. So if poor Johnny died from sampling the root of the tall plant with the pretty, lacy flowers, the whole tribe could steer clear.

Your mind's ability to form all these relationships is invaluable! But language can quickly backfire on you. For instance, say your grandmother has a mango tree, and you think of her whenever you're eating a mango. When she suddenly passes away, the mere sight of a mango can trigger a wave of grief.

Imagine a detailed mind map with many connections linked to various objects, events, thoughts, and feelings. Any one situation could trigger any of those associations. Your dog can't make those associations, at least not to the level of complexity you can. In a way, she's blessed not to have this human language to deal with. If at any point we have a negative association with a neutral object, all the things connected to that object can bring up uncomfortable thoughts and feelings.

So we live in a language minefield where any object can trigger various chains of thought. We have limited power over what comes up, because associations form during our upbringing and ongoing life experiences. That's also why trying to add a new link to an existing chain—like when you practice positive self-talk—can have a paradoxical effect, reminding you of that negative thought you're actively trying to quiet.

If you look at how these associations show up with negative self-talk, you'll see that your mind can conjure complex negative associations about yourself from any neutral situation. For instance, a work email gets blasted about a new managerial position that would be a promotion. For a hot second, you consider applying, but a memory immediately emerges. You recall your annual review two years ago. The boss highlighted your potential for being a manager and discussed areas you could improve. Your mind disregards the positive feedback (it was an overall positive review), instead thinking, *There's no way I have what it takes to apply.*

That memory and negative self-talk influence you to feel unworthy. Now suppose other memories further reinforce the feeling of unworthiness, such as being in group projects in college where you were never the leader. Then the thought comes to mind, *I've always been more of a follower than a leader. I'm just not leadership material.*

Your mind associated a neutral event and traced it back to past failures (recent past and a long time ago). No wonder you don't want to apply for that promotion! You don't want to risk going down that unworthiness path again if you don't get the job. Your inner critic convinces you it's protecting you from potential failure and from feeling that pain of unworthiness. And that makes sense. But it's not conducive to living your best life.

Now you've seen that your mind can work against you because of its unique ability to relate any object to another—making a relationship between two seemingly incompatible things. And that relationship can go on to shape the way you think and behave in the present. If you don't believe me, let's do a quick exercise.

Exercise (Adapted from Hayes and Smith 2005)

- Take out your chosen note-keeper. Write any noun—person, place, or thing.
- On another line, write another noun.
- Answer the following questions:
    - How is the first noun like the second noun?

- How is the first noun better than the second noun?
- How is the first noun the parent of the second noun? This might feel trickier, but see if you can answer it.

Isn't that neat, that your mind can take two random objects and somehow find a way to connect them? But it's not so awesome when we are part of the equation. Our minds can find a comparison between ourselves and anyone else. In no time at all, your mind can easily think of someone smarter, more attractive, and more successful than you. Ouch!

Chapter 5

When Is the Inner Critic Born?

Early in life, you start to understand that you're a separate individual from those strange figures making weird faces at you. Researchers believe this starts as early as age four or five months, with particular skills developing even before that age (Shaffer 2005). Once you understand this, you begin making a coherent narrative about who you are.

As a child, you might focus more on describing yourself by age, sex, physical attributes, likes, dislikes, and possessions. The older you get, the more this self-story expands. It includes psychological descriptions: personality traits, your roles, and self-judgments.

Your self-story might include both positive and negative thoughts about yourself. And inevitably, part of that narrative will be a self-story that doesn't paint you in the best light. Your mind doesn't care if the story is accurate; it just wants a story that makes sense, even if part of it is hurtful to bear. Your mind usually deals in black and white and steers clear of gray areas, especially regarding your sense of self.

Another factor influencing your self-story's development is the mind's complex associations, discussed in chapter 4. This can lead to comparing yourself to others. Traits or faults on which the mind judges you as "less than" compared to others can become part of your self-story.

Or worse, even an idealized version of yourself can become a standard that you constantly compare and judge yourself against. When you're not hitting these ideals, that can also contribute to your negative self-talk. Isn't that something?

Your mind can conjure a "perfect" version of you, engage in constant comparison, and find you lacking. (Your dog doesn't do that to you.) This can be pervasive for those who struggle with perfectionism and have rigid and high expectations for themselves.

Your story of who you are can also be influenced by your view on how others view you. If you have experiences that made you feel rejected (and didn't have your own in-group to be part of), this experience can be added to your self-story as another reason you're less than others.

Finally, it may come as no surprise, but the types of relationships you had with your caretakers can also play a vital factor in your negative self-talk. Two significant determinants include how critical they were and how responsive to your emotional needs—whether and how they provided affection and nurturance and were receptive to your emotional experiences—as shown in the chart (LeJeune 2016).

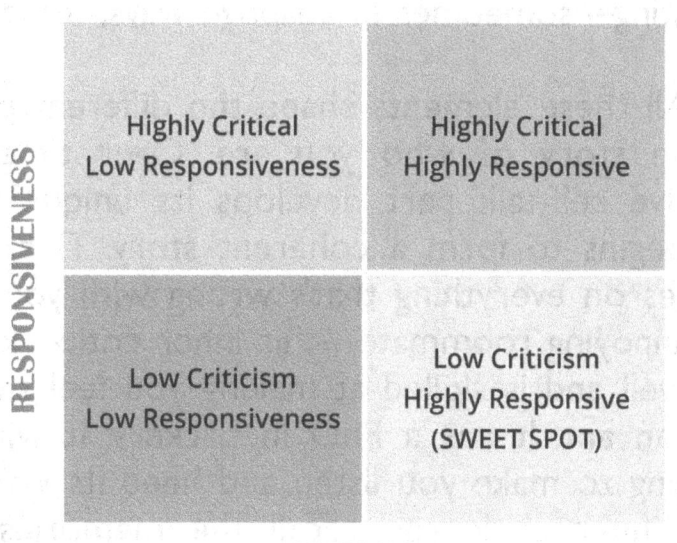

If you experienced any combination of these factors outside of the sweet spot, it could have played a role in developing your inner critic. Qualities you were criticized for while growing up can be a sensitive spot and be part of your self-narrative.

My clients often express confusion when they have a loud inner critic but nothing "bad" has happened in their lives. If your caretakers struggled to be warm and nurturing, it could have affected you, even if you didn't experience trauma. The goal here isn't to demonize your caretakers. Some of us indeed had parents who behaved in ways they shouldn't have. But many parents don't intend to cause pain to their kids. They're simply flawed humans with their own negative self-talk, potential inner critics, and life experiences that contribute to their parenting—sometimes in adaptive ways, sometimes not.

All these elements shape the different pieces of the story of who you are. Over time, the negative self-talk part develops its unique voice and begins to form a coherent story. This story focuses on everything that's wrong with you. And this annoying roommate—this inner critic—knows you well and is skilled at making you feel smaller than an ant. It has a PhD in trickery. It will use anything to make you listen and heed its warning. Your inner critic can recall the memories you desperately want to forget. It whispers doubts, rules, and traps that keep you guessing and powerless. It uses all its knowledge about who you are, and it can turn the tables on you.

To be fair to the inner critic, sometimes it's trying to protect you in its own screwy way. One reason your inner critic developed is to explain certain situations in your life. For instance, you might have felt confused by your mother's inconsistency in expressing love and affection toward you. Rather than stay confused, your mind might tell a story about who you are and what you might've done to deserve that treatment. Such as, *There's something wrong with me; that's why she's MIA sometimes. I'm not lovable enough.*

This provides an explanation for your mother's inconsistency and painful absences. Granted, it depends on a distortion of the facts. But once this story has taken root, your mind will look for evidence to reinforce it. Let's say you have a spat with your friend in middle school; your mind will say, *You see, something is wrong with you!* Or let's say when you're in your first serious romantic relationship in college, your partner gets busy with finals and spends less time with you. This fires up your anxiety. Your mind conjures the following to explain it: *Uh-oh! It's happening again. He's tired of me. He's started to figure out that I'm not special enough. It's me again!*

Even if this story is painfully familiar to you over the years, it's still hard to deal with. So you might knowingly or unknowingly engage in ways to prevent this narrative from getting activated. Let's go back to the middle-school version of you. You decided that developing a pattern of pleasing others is the best way to ensure this "I am unlovable story" doesn't get triggered. You decided to swallow your frustration with your friend, apologize, and focus on your friend's needs before your own. From then on, you made it a point to embody that cool, go-with-the-flow friend who is always so damn agreeable! And your inner critic was satisfied, because it also wants to protect you from getting hurt again.

Or let's say that instead of turning toward pleasing others, you decide to avoid pursuing genuine relationships. Your mind reasons that this is the best way to prevent anyone from seeing that fatal flaw again. Occasionally you sense something missing from your life (authentic connection with others). But your inner critic reminds you: *No! Relationships are not safe! They will eventually notice that you're not enough. Don't go there!*

In a twisted way, this is also your mind's way of shielding you, even if it's not optimal. It says all these nasty things about you and orders you to listen to them—to protect yourself. It glosses over the pain of missing out on pursuing life's meaningful (and risky) avenues. Your mind is comfortable with the trade-offs because its primary focus is to keep you safe.

To be clear, sometimes your inner critic is not trying to protect you. It's simply triggering this deep and painful self-hatred in you. Its goal isn't to protect you but to punish you, because your mind agrees: *I deserve it.* This can look like your mind trying to protect you, because the way you engage (either to please or avoid) can be the same. But your inner critic's intentions here are different. These instances tend to feel harsher and more painful, because your mind tells you that you deserve to be whipped (metaphorically).

A word of caution and compassion here: This self-loathing can arise from a history of trauma, abuse, or a combination of factors. Regardless of how frequently this happens (occasionally or chronically), it's excruciating. The more you recognize it, the better you can work on it. Give yourself tremendous amounts of kindness, forgiveness, and grace if you have more instances of self-loathing—because it could take a bit more work to become flexible. But you'll get there if you persist and treat yourself with kindness and patience.

One way to gain the upper hand with your inner critic is to get familiar with it instead of trying to avoid or tune out what it says. You want to understand what this inner critic uses against you.

Exercise

We're diving into the deep end here. I'm sorry. At no point did I say this journey would be easy—but I do hope it will be worthwhile.
- Jot down everything your inner critic says about you. Get to the core of what it says that sucks you in and feels difficult to write down. Trust me: Getting to know your inner critic is essential—becoming familiar with the jabs it throws and its hold on your life.
- List what experiences could have influenced your self-story, including your relationship with your parents/caretakers and critical events. Note: The goal isn't to focus only on relationships you felt were lacking. It's helpful

to recall relationships that include some warmth.

Chapter 6

Your Inner Critic Is Not Living Rent-Free in Your Head

Jessica had tears in her eyes and a painful expression of humiliation as she listed all the ways her inner critic has interfered in her life:
- It has her not believing that she's worthy enough to have a stable relationship. She settles for guys who treat her less than great.
- That nagging voice in her head—*What if they say no? What if they decide to let you go? You'll never actually get it*—keeps her from asking for a raise. Even though she's been working as a temporary supervisor for five months.
- It forces her to yo-yo diet, hoping to find the diet to help her finally shed weight. Convincing her that only then will she feel better about herself.
- It leaves her struggling to set limits with her sister, who always asks for last-minute favors or to borrow money. Like when she asked to borrow money for a "great deal on tickets

to Coachella. Oh, and by the way, can you dog-sit Sparky for me too?"

I hear these and similar client stories when we explore how the inner critic interferes in their lives. It can be a painful exercise to recognize how you move through life in response to your inner critic. On the other hand, it might not seem that outlandish, because you've had a lifetime of experience obeying all the rules and commandments it screams at you.

Ultimately, living with your inner critic isn't the problem. Recall its role in trying to protect you from the potential pain of rejection or failure, as in Jessica's case with her elusive promotion. You don't have control over the inner critic's existence, because it's hardwired to keep you "safe" from physical or emotional pain. But you can learn to react differently to your inner critic and reduce its interference in living your life.

It's normal to try a range of behaviors to control, get rid of, or appease your inner critic, because otherwise it causes you a ton of pain. You're not alone in having an innate desire and instinct to silence your inner critic or give in. Listen, even single-cell organisms will move away from pain. The catch is that you typically pay a price when you'll do *anything* to respond to or eliminate the inner critic—whether that price is wasting your time, energy, or effort, or missing out on things that matter.

One way to think about the critic and how to relate to it is by differentiating between *clean* and *dirty* pain. Clean pain is the pain associated with living or the pain of presence. I often tell my clients that if they live long enough, they will encounter some form of pain. What kind of pain it is will depend on them as individuals and their lived experiences. It could range from the crippling fear of making a mistake, to grief over losing their grandfather, to the trauma of surviving a horrific car accident or sadness and betrayal over an unexpected divorce. Whatever your clean pain happens to be, it's the trade-off for being alive.

Dirty pain, on the other hand, is everything you do to try to control or avoid feeling the clean pain—which inevitably comes with a cost. Take a preceding example to see the potential associated dirty pain:

- *Crippling fear of making mistakes:* You spend too much time worrying about doing the "right" thing. You may miss opportunities until you're sure it's the best decision. You spend too much time and energy exhaustively researching a project at the expense of time with your little ones.
- *Grief over losing your grandfather:* You avoid talking to your mom about him due to the associated pain, but you miss an opportunity

to connect. You might even trash all his pictures since the grief is too much.
- *Trauma after a car accident:* You develop a fear of being on a highway. You go out of your way to stay on the local streets and don't venture anywhere you can't get to locally, limiting your movement. You miss going to your niece's first recital because you'd have to take a highway.
- *Sadness and betrayal over a divorce:* You declare you can't trust any man because of a painful divorce. To avoid feeling sadness, grief, anger, and betrayal again, you make up a rigid story about the male gender to protect yourself. But you lose the opportunity for new relationships and connections.

Dirty pain is the pain of absence. The pain that shows up when you focus on trying to avoid or control the pain associated with the clean pain. The challenge with dirty pain is that you might experience some relief when you avoid the clean pain. But you conveniently overlook its costs or lie to yourself. You might feel relief that you don't have to drive on the highway to go to the recital. But after the relief, you feel worse because you missed seeing your niece dancing her little butt off in her bright orange tutu. Those feelings that show up, that absence you experience—that there is the dirty pain.

Don't be dismayed if you have more dirty pain thanks to your inner critic. Part of your work through this book is to shift the focus to reducing those instances in your life. By making bold and scary choices to live your life according to what matters to you. Not in the service of avoiding the clean pain, but in the service of your values. To become more comfortable with the clean pain, particularly the one associated with your inner critic.

In the following few chapters, we will further explore the costs of the inner critic in different areas of your life. Let's start here first.

Exercise

This exercise is about understanding the unique costs of listening to or trying to avoid your inner critic. This will be your master list. You might add more later, so keep this handy.
- List how the inner critic has influenced your life, just as Jessica did when we met.
- What reactions show up for you as you list these? Sit with those reactions if you can, even if they are uncomfortable.

Chapter 7

Relationship with Self

The inner critic is a pro at making you feel like crap. It makes you question whether you're a worthy human being, deserving of love, affection, and the pursuit of your values. Basically, it triggers the feeling of shame. Researcher and author Brené Brown defines shame as "the intensely painful feeling or experience of believing that we are flawed and therefore unworthy of love, belonging, and connection" (2021).

We can feel this sense of being flawed for any number of reasons.

If at the root of your inner critic's commentary is this constant sense that you're not good enough, it can appear in every area of your life. Because you live with a soul-sucking sense that something is crucially wrong with you, it can show up when you're trying to advance your career, start dating again after being ghosted, begin a workout routine, or when you snap at your kid. Typically, it shows up when you do things in areas that matter to you.

Your inner critic also makes you doubt yourself and your choices. It chimes in at all hours, particularly in those wee hours of the night when you're trying to sleep! It does its running commentary on your choices, highlighting past mistakes and warning you about future mistakes. Then it likes to link that back to past failures to ensure you remember not to repeat them.

So you live with a cloud of self-doubt and a lack of confidence in your ability to make the best decisions. You struggle to trust your decision-making skills and to know what's best for you. You seek advice from others because maybe *they* know what's best for you. And if you listen to them, well, at least the results aren't your fault; you were just following directions.

This also means that even when you tune out all the inner critic's noise and sit with your gut feeling, you still might betray yourself—to please others, because your inner critic is making you doubt yourself again. This leads you to live a life based on obedience to others rather than one where you're driving the bus. And when you do pause and reflect on your choices, you might feel a sense of despair because a part of you knows you're basing decisions on what you "should" do or what others think is right versus what feels true to you.

The other messed-up part is that your inner critic is never satisfied, even if you're not making mistakes. It will still find something to make a note of, to make sure you're "being careful"—or, if you have been obeying it, it'll warn you not to do anything to mess up. And contemplating any action that it considers outside of a safe window of tolerance can be risky, as it will be quick to discourage you from following through. This slowly erodes your confidence, and you believe you can't handle difficulties.

Ultimately, you end up in a lose-lose relationship with your inner critic. No matter what decisions you make, whether they turn out well or not, it can still find something to criticize. Then you have the extra baggage of knowing that you decided based on trying to please or quiet your inner critic rather than what you knew was right for you. So now you're dealing with that painful self-awareness of missing out on living your life according to your values.

Think about how you typically interact with your inner critic. Do you believe it and try to quiet it down by pleasing it? Or maybe you take a more combative stance, trying to yell back at it or endlessly going back and forth to prove it wrong, like you're in a debate-style competition. Or do you grin and bear it—holding your breath while it spews all these hurtful things at you?

Whether you feel a constant need to obey, or to combat, or to bear it, your inner critic's influence leaves you in an exhausting adversarial relationship with it. You're struggling with an ever-present part of yourself. Because as much as it might pain you to admit or accept it, your inner critic is still a part of you. And you lack self-compassion or acceptance for this part of yourself.

That can generalize to lacking a sense of self-appreciation for yourself overall. It may feel like the inner critic is this bigger-than-life presence that tries to hog the spotlight and takes up all the air in the room. And you put so much effort into keeping it out that you forget to tend to the other parts of yourself.

You're not alone in struggling with this part of yourself. In my experience, this feeling that you're not enough is a common agonizing experience. But we don't do a good job of talking about it. Most of us walk around with a sense that we're not good enough, for whatever reason, but there's an unwritten rule to keep quiet. It feels too vulnerable and scary to let people in on what causes us to feel less than or different. Ironically, shame festers when we don't talk about it.

It reminds me of a workshop by Kelly G. Wilson that I attended in graduate school. He handed out an index card and said, "Write down that thing about you that makes you feel so off or different. The one that, when it hits, feels so painful to acknowledge. Then consider how long you've known this about yourself."

I can't exactly recall what I wrote down, but I know whatever it was, it was something that made me feel less than. But one thing became clear to me as I glanced around. Almost everyone had their version of this thing that made them feel less than, unlovable, unworthy. I was not alone in my experience, just as you're not alone in your experience.

Exercise

Now let's investigate the inner critic's role in your relationship with yourself.
- Revisit your responses to the master list in chapter 6. Home in on the specific costs to your relationship with yourself. Add any more costs that come to mind.
- Consider how you respond to the inner critic when it comments on you. What are the costs of any of these reactions?

Chapter 8

Relationship with Others

A significant way the inner critic shows up is by wreaking havoc in your relationship with others, whether that's romantic partners, friends, or family members. It convinces you that everything it says about you is accurate. If you believe something is incurably wrong and impacts your lovability, that can cause you to engage differently with others.

Broadly speaking, the inner critic can convince you to anxiously pursue relationships in your life. By "anxiously pursue," I mean any of the following and more:
- Feeling unable to be single because it's too uncomfortable to be with your thoughts and feelings
- Frantically looking for external validation to quiet the noise in your head temporarily
- Pursuing unavailable partners
- Ignoring glaring red flags
- Settling for partners you don't truly connect with because your mind says, *This is the best you can do*

This applies not only to romantic partners but also to relationships with friends and family members. Each has its own dynamics. With friends, you could end up in one-sided friendships, feel taken for granted, and have difficulties setting limits. You may outgrow certain friendships but refuse to accept the need to sever ties, for fear of ending up friendless.

With family members, there are some deeper entrenched patterns. Your inner critic might have specific rules about your family dynamics that it made up a long time ago, which it commands you to follow rigidly; for example:

- *If Mom is mad at me, I did something wrong. I must ensure she doesn't get angry with me.*
- *My brother is the responsible one, and I'm the black sheep. They don't trust me to get it together; that must mean I'm a loser.*

As a result, your inner critic convinces you to try to earn love and affection within these relationships, even when it's clear that may never come to pass. You might forgo your needs to stay in relationships with certain family members. You may lack limits even when it impinges on your time, money, and energy demands.

On the other end of the spectrum, your inner critic might persuade you that relationships with others are unsafe. If you let others in, they might see the parts of yourself you consider unbearable, and you will end up hurt. So it's much easier to build and maintain these solid walls to keep others out.

For many of us, that looks like not pursuing romantic relationships or even friendships. Or, if you do, there's a clear mandate to keep those relationships at a surface level, never allowing anyone to get too close or to see your more vulnerable side because that feels too scary. You might even say all the right things, but when it truly matters, you withdraw and shut down.

A loud inner critic can make some people more prone to look for potential signs of rejection. You might interpret constructive feedback from a partner as rejection or the potential for it. Additionally, this propensity to be on the lookout can impact how you react when receiving mild signs of rejection. You're quicker to lash out, shut down, get angry, and trigger the inner critic to start up. The problem is, this can hurt your relationships with others.

To be clear, it might not be that cut and dry. Your way of engaging can change from relationship to relationship. You might be much better at setting limits with friendships, but you cave when it comes to your family. Perhaps you anxiously cling to your ex-girlfriend but withdraw from your current relationship. The goal is to understand what drives you to behave the way you do in your relationships. Then you can decide if those behaviors cultivate the types of relationships you want. How you engage can also change within a relationship at different stages.

Exercise

This exercise will target the inner critic's role in your relationship with others.

- Return to your master list in chapter 6 and focus on the impact on your relationships. Add any more that come to mind.
- Break down these instances into past and current relationships. For relationships in the past, what role did the inner critic play? Were there instances when it paid to listen to your inner critic? It's completely normal if there have been.
- Now look at your inner critic's role in your current relationships, and consider whether it's influencing a lack of relationships. Consider how your inner critic's voice is or isn't working to support establishing the relationships you want.
- Imagine for a moment what it would mean if you could have different, more significant relationships with others. What qualities and personal values would you want your relationships to reflect?

Chapter 9

Relationship with Achievements

Your inner critic convinces you to avoid pursuing meaningful things, including achievement-oriented activities. Achievements can be anything you value and dedicate time to outside your relationships. Activities include education, career, leisure, side hustles, volunteer work, and more. To be clear, these are not dependent on status, but actions you believe are worthy of committing your energy to.

The inner critic will make you question whether you have what it takes to pursue these, especially when it requires a significant change, like deciding to return to school or doing a career 180. Your inner critic will highlight past failures, focus on qualities you lack, and encourage you to stick with what you already know. When you do try something new, it might trigger major imposter syndrome, an offshoot of the inner critic. You feel like a fraud, downplay any past achievements, and believe you're just not capable.

When it comes to achievements, your inner critic can encourage you to stay on the sidelines of your life, rather than risk failing and getting bombarded by negative self-talk. So you decide not to become a nurse; instead, you become an accountant. You've always been good at numbers anyway.

There's nothing wrong with being an accountant—you enjoy it—yet that *what if?* thought is swirling in your mind. Or you've made peace with your decision, but it's essential to recognize whether you're still letting fear dictate other choices in your life.

On the other hand, your inner critic might convince you that you can silence it by accumulating more gold stars. It tells you the only way to prove you're worthy is by continuing to be the best, going above and beyond, and never resting from the treadmill of achievement. You may lose sight of being present and enjoying engaging in something that matters because you focus only on the outcome. Oh, and it doesn't matter if you're at the point of burnout. Your inner critic will deceive you—it tells you it will all be worth it in the long run, and you'll get to rest and feel worthy later.

When you're promoted or recognized and feel a sense of accomplishment—that shuts the inner critic up, temporarily. Yet for some reason the feeling doesn't last. It starts up again in a couple of days, weeks, or (if you're lucky) months. It tells you it doesn't count, and you must work harder for the next thing. The crappy part is that you keep believing all its lies.

Perhaps your inner critic gets selective, allowing you to pursue certain accepted avenues. It says you're allowed to dedicate your time and effort to being a mother and an attorney, but it's selfish to find time for hobbies or time with friends. Other areas are off-limits because specific rules tell you it's selfish to take care of yourself.

Exercise

As before, revisit your growing master list. Focus on the costs to your relationship with achievements.
- Consider all types of achievements through your schooling, careers, or outside ventures, past or present.
- If you've missed any, add them under this achievement umbrella.

Oof! I know listing all the costs in the different areas of your life in the last chapters may have been rough. I hope you see the damage that negative self-talk can do in convincing you to live a small, safe life. The more you listen to your inner critic—whether to silence it, control it, or heed its warnings—the more you miss out on living. This can foster a sense of regret and awareness that you could do more, handle more, and be more resilient than your inner critic wants to give you credit for.

By never taking risks, you may miss out on the big moments. Those moments of true intimacy when you risk being vulnerable and your partner reaches out and reaffirms that they love you anyway. You miss out on that moment when you feel empowered after leaving your safe job to pursue a side hustle that fills you with joy and purpose.

As you go through this book, you will gain the skills you need to help you become willing to make these bold choices.

Chapter 10

Your Inner Critic Has Its Moments

By this point you probably have some negative thoughts about your inner critic! And I get it—it's only natural, when you've identified its impact on your life (from making you feel less than glamorous to encouraging you to wall yourself off from relationships). But I don't want you to have a one-sided view of your inner critic, because it was created to make sense of the world around you. A negative story is better than no story (that is, uncertainty). Your brain does not like ambiguous scenarios, because then it can't plan to protect and keep you safe.

Consider it like an overprotective parent who has good intentions but comes off as critical and overbearing. Your inner critic tells you negative things about yourself to protect you from the potential dangers of not heeding its warnings. For instance, if your inner critic constantly comments on your appearance and advises you that you must look a certain way to be lovable or accepted, it's trying to make sure you understand the potential for rejection if you don't fit these standards. Your inner critic may say things like:

- *You're too thin; your butt is flatter than a pancake.*
- *You're too fat. Have you stepped on the scale lately?*
- *You're not muscular enough; others think you look weak.*
- *You're too old. Have you seen all those wrinkles on your face?*

Your harsh inner critic encourages you to fix all these supposed problems, so you won't get hurt. It might encourage you to:

- Do some extra squats so you can fill out those jeans
- Go back on that restrictive diet so you can start dating again
- Lift heavy weights so you can bulk up
- Have the new state-of-the-art unregulated and risky skincare product injected into your face so you can look younger

Regardless of whether these behaviors are healthy or unhealthy, it's clear that the underlying intention is entirely off base. Your inner critic sorely misses the mark and fails to realize that your self-worth is not linked to your appearance (which is hard to buy into in our appearance-obsessed culture). But your inner critic wants to keep you safe from others commenting on or rejecting you because of your appearance—to protect you from the painful feelings that can appear if this happens.

The irony is that you have no control over others' opinions or reactions to you. You can do everything your inner critic tells you to do and still get negative feedback. But it still wants to feel some control and wants you to believe you can do something to prevent hurt.

There may have been instances when you've listened to your inner critic and it helped somehow. For example, after a difficult breakup, it told you, *You see, you don't have what it takes to be in a relationship; don't share that side of you again.* That caused you to take time to heal and learn from the relationship. It also stopped you from rushing into another one before you were ready. You focused on deepening friendships instead. So listening to that feedback did help you in the short term.

But at some point it stopped helping. You got to the point where you had processed your feelings about it and started to miss dating. But those thoughts from your inner critic induced fear and avoidance of dating because you believed you'd get hurt again or rejected.

To be clear, I'm not saying what the inner critic says is true. Sometimes listening to it has been helpful, but it can stop being useful when it keeps you from pursuing your values. Suppose you buy into the belief that you don't have what it takes to be vulnerable, but your value is to be in a loving, affectionate, intimate relationship. In that case, your inner critic is impeding that goal.

If you zoom out a bit, you can gain the perspective to realize that everything that makes up the inner critic is a part of who you are. Maybe it's a painful part, perhaps created during some tough times in your life, but it's still as much a part of you as the parts that you boast about; it deserves equal acceptance and compassion, but not control.

As I mentioned in chapter 5, sometimes your inner self does not have your best intentions in mind and primarily tries to punish you. This might be hard to spot, but it feels different—more inflexible, and based on a history of painful (potentially even traumatic) experiences. Its underlying intentions are not related to protecting you or keeping you safe.

Exercise

Step away from the content of the hurtful thoughts your inner critic aims at you and consider:
- What are your inner critic's ultimate intentions?
- Are any of these intentions intended to protect you (even if it goes about it in all the wrong ways)?
- Have there been any instances where the inner critic did protect you?
- Similarly, are there any instances when the experience feels different, and you can sense

that your inner critic is just trying to punish you?

I hope you now have a more nuanced view of your inner critic. It's not just a slimeball; sometimes it's a slimeball with a heart, trying to protect you. The goal is for you to avoid having a rigid view of your inner critic as all bad and banishing it to a deep, dark corner of your mind. If you instead allow it more space to walk around, you can decide how to react to what it says about you and not get too hooked on its specific contents. Then decide from a place of your values how you want to engage with it and whether you wish to listen to it. Perhaps you can even give it some kindness. Yup, I said kindness. More on that later.

Chapter 11

You've Tried It All, with No Success

Matt looked at me with desperation and annoyance.

I'd asked, "Have any of these strategies worked to end the critical thoughts completely?"

He grudgingly admitted, "No, I still hear these thoughts all the time! That's why I'm here, for you to get them to stop! There must be something wrong with me!"

Matt is not alone in believing that something is fatally wrong with him for having these thoughts constantly pop up. This all-or-nothing attitude is typical, and there are several good reasons why.

Western society's prevalent school of thought is that we should always be happy and positive. This cultural norm fosters our avoidance strategy because it perpetuates the belief that something is wrong with you if you're not. When you have an uncomfortable feeling (typically labeled a negative emotion), you may notice labeling the feeling as "not okay." You believe that having these feelings must mean something is wrong with you.

Marketing firms capitalize on our intrinsic negative self-talk and feelings of inadequacy by encouraging us to find the "solution"—be that purchasing the newest car model, going on a life-altering vacation, or buying that five-day detox system. Again, nothing wrong with engaging in any of these behaviors, but I want you to consider the various factors influencing your decisions.

This feel-good perspective isn't prevalent only in the mass media. Many grew up surrounded by individuals struggling with uncomfortable thoughts and feelings. So, what happens?

You are twelve years old and feel a sense of emptiness because you don't have anyone to sit with at lunch. When you share this with your mother, she immediately goes into fix-it mode: "Let's see if I can call Jenny's mom to see if Jenny can sit with you tomorrow." Or your mom listens but tells you, "Don't stress it, honey. This won't matter in a couple of years." What your mom's trying to do isn't wrong, but at that moment you feel invalidated. You get the implied message: *This situation shouldn't cause me to feel these uncomfortable feelings and thoughts. Maybe something is wrong with me because this makes me feel bad. I should fix it!*

Or your caregivers tell you it's okay to feel all the feelings, but they model something else regarding their own emotional experiences: They always try to be okay, and they never cry or acknowledge difficult moments. I'm not talking about parents in crisis mode. I'm talking about those who adhere to a strict mandate never to display uncomfortable feelings in front of their children. They tend to model avoidance rather than making room for feelings or acknowledging that it's okay for them to have these internal experiences. And this teaches you to do the same.

There's an unvoiced rule in all these messages: Negative thoughts or feelings must be "fixed," making them inherently wrong. If you pause and think about this, you'll realize that's nuts!

I mean, part of the deal of being human is that you feel pain. There are no ifs, ands, or buts about it. What, how, and when pain is triggered is unique to your story, biology, and lived experiences, but clean pain is guaranteed. The dirty pain is optional. Part of what sustains the dirty pain is all these messages.

Another popular message: You should have more control over your internal experiences than you do. This message is even touted in some popular psychological theories. A great example is the popular notions related to self-esteem. You will hear that one way to achieve high self-esteem is to transform negative self-talk into positive self-talk. So if you think, *I'm such a loser!*, you would work on challenging or changing that thought to a more helpful and balanced perspective, such as *I'm not a loser, and here's why.*

Again, if that works for you, you keep doing what works. The potential problem with this approach is that you spend time and energy trying to eliminate all these negative thoughts about yourself, but they keep coming back. As noted in chapter 4, it triggers other thoughts that make a chain reaction, like when you see the job email and think you don't have it takes to be a leader. Picture a spiderweb: One thought can link to all these intricate associations.

The mainstream view is that you *should have more control* over these negative thoughts. In essence, you should be able to eliminate these thoughts completely. This also applies to other internal experiences, including emotions and physical sensations.

Your mind does not have a huge red Delete button that you can press immediately when you have a negative thought about yourself. Some activities—like drinking, bingeing, or doing any engrossing activity to numb yourself—can press a temporary pause button, but that also comes with a cost.

No wonder Matt had bought into all these myths and his problem-solving mind had gone to work to end these critical thoughts. The more strategies he tried, with limited long-term success, the sadder and more hopeless he felt. Because no matter what he did, the inner critic eventually crept back. He was convinced that something was wrong with him for continuing to have these painful internal experiences, which further added to his pain and struggle.

Exercise

Remember that it's normal to want to move away from pain as Matt tried to do. And it's also helpful to understand the chain of events that follows.
- Start by listing everything you've done to eliminate or avoid your negative self-talk and the associated inner experiences.
- Consider whether each of these strategies has worked. I don't mean to eliminate the thoughts, but have they worked by helping you engage in behaviors that bring you closer to a meaningful life?

If you conclude that these strategies haven't worked to help you live an authentic life, then you might feel like Matt. A mixture of frustration and hopelessness. But you might also notice feeling a little sense of relief. Relief that you don't have a programming error—that it's natural and expected to have negative thoughts and associated experiences. It also frees up more of your energy and time to focus on the things you do have control of. Which, in essence, is what you do with your body and your behaviors.

One way to think about this is to imagine you're back in the fifth grade and getting ready for Field Day. You're on the far superior blue team. You get to school and start with a game of tug of war.

Suddenly you realize you're in a nightmare: It's just you against your personal bogeyman, and there's a vast, gaping hole between the two of you that one of you could tumble into to their death. This bogeyman has razor-sharp yellow teeth, red bulging eyes, horns dark as night, and thick talons. And worse, he spews all these mean and hateful things to the precious fifth-grade version of you.

Here you are, confronted with the Herculean task of fighting your bogeyman. You pick up the rope and use all your strength. You pull and pull. Soon, though, your arms get sore, the rope bites into your palms, and your sneakers lose traction.

You reach the point where you're exhausted and recognize that your efforts have been futile. You finally decide to drop the freaking rope in defeat. And, unexpectedly, while the bogeyman gets louder and more prominent, you realize he can't reach you. He can pull the rope, but that's all he can do to bridge the distance between you.

As you stand there looking at him, you start to see him from all these new angles. The longer you stare, the more you realize he's not so scary.

You might feel a sense of fear, desperation, and hopelessness when dropping the rope. But after that hopelessness, you may realize there's another way.

PART 2

How to Find Your Inner Ally

Up to this point, through this book, you've come to better understand negative self-talk and why it's an experience you share with all humans. I hope that by understanding the factors involved in your relationship with your inner critic, you feel validated that you're not alone or defective for having these internal experiences.

I also expect you might feel frustrated and sad as you've dived into the costs and the hold it's had on your life. You've acknowledged that sometimes listening to your inner critic may have worked in your favor, and other times it hasn't. And you're getting a sense of needing to pivot in those moments.

You're right—there is another path. Once you've dropped the rope, you've freed yourself up to live your life, knowing your bogeyman will still find ways to follow you. But if you're ready to do something different, because you're done listening to its idle threats, then this part 2 is for you!

This part of the book guides you through tools and processes from acceptance and commitment therapy (ACT), a form of psychotherapy focused on helping you live your life based on what's meaningful to you (your values) and helping you learn some new skills to help you get unstuck from sticky thoughts, feelings, urges, physical sensations, or memories.

ACT focuses on making changes in the service of living your life, regardless of whether a thought is true, whether an uncomfortable feeling shows up, or any other factor tries to get in the way. As we've learned, we all struggle with our moments of clean pain and moments of heartache that life events, internal experiences, or both can trigger. That's just part of life. Luckily for us, ACT has research to back up its effectiveness in working with these issues; most of the concepts in part I are from the theory and research in ACT.

As a therapist, I've continued to use ACT in my work because I've seen how it can help clients change their lives. Of course, not without bumps and detours on the road. I've seen people light up when engaging in values work and when they realize any behavior can move them either away from or closer to what matters to them.

I've seen people be kinder to themselves and believe they matter, even if their negative self-talk persists. I've seen people find the courage to leave their safe but deeply unsatisfying jobs, commit to sobriety, put themselves out there again, and be willing to have difficult conversations with loved ones. All those moments have reinforced my desire to share this with more people.

If you're still on the fence, that's completely understandable. I know the powerful hold that negative self-talk can have in your life, so maybe you're not sold. I still encourage you to dive into part 2 with a curious mind and an attitude of experimentation. You don't have to buy into everything, but at least commit to trying out some of the new tools in this section. See what works. Keep those, and drop the rest. Again, my goal is for you to do what works in the service of your values.

I hope you start to stretch moment by moment by trying out some of the new strategies to find your inner ally, as described in part 2.

Chapter 12

Creating Distance from Your Thoughts

One of the most significant components of negative self-talk (it may be the biggest) is your thoughts. The good news: You don't need to spend more time and energy figuring out how to eliminate all those pesky thoughts. You've already tried that with little to no success. And you don't have to focus on having more positive thoughts, either. Instead, the aim is to change your relationship with your negative thoughts. Instead of trying to delete your thoughts, the focus will be on creating distance from them.

The thing is, thoughts are just thoughts. That concept might sound extremely simple. But when I clarify to clients that they don't have to listen to everything their mind says about a situation, the world, or themselves, they typically look confused—as if this is a new realization, that they can do something different, despite their thoughts. Even more so when it comes to some old repetitive thoughts that have been around for a long time. They might say, "Yeah, okay, I don't have to listen to the thought to buy that shiny object." But when I tell them it also applies to that old thought *No one will ever be able to meet my needs*, they look at me suspiciously.

The problem isn't that your mind is thinking; that's part of its job description. The issue is that you believe or get hooked by everything it produces. Or when a thought shows up, you don't realize it is there, influencing how you feel or engage. It's as if you're viewing the world through a filter but aren't even aware that the color has changed.

Luckily, just by realizing this, you've started to get a one-up on your mind. You've learned an essential hack in reining in your mind rather than feeling at the mercy of your thoughts. There are endless ways to approach this skill, but it is all about seeing thoughts for what they are: just words strung together that form sentences and convey a specific meaning.

Think about it. If you don't read Chinese and this was texted to you:

你是一文不值的垃圾

you probably wouldn't be able to mount a reaction (other than puzzlement).

But if you were texted, "You are worthless garbage," that's more likely to stir something up. Because you're fluent in this language, these symbols strung together mean something to you. Those other symbols don't, so you don't get all riled up.

The more you see that thoughts are just symbols conveying a message, the more you can decide whether heeding the message works for you.

How do you go about doing this? Let's look at some tools you can apply right now.

Exercise: I'm Noticing...

How can two words be so simple but so powerful? One quick and easy way to build this skill is to do the following. Grab your notes apparatus.

Start by identifying a thought that you're having right now.

Whatever thought you wrote down, read it several times and repeat it yourself. See what that feels like.

Now rewrite the sentence but add this first:

I'm having the thought

Try this version and see what it's like when you read and repeat it. Do you feel more or less attached to the initial thought?

Let's take it one step further. Now, add more to the beginning of the sentence by writing:

I'm noticing I'm having the thought

Repeat this phrase a couple of times. See how this lands. Again, how attached do you feel to the initial sentence?

If you feel less attached, you can keep using this small technique. So next time your mind tells you, *You're such a loser!* you can remind yourself to add, *I'm noticing I'm having the thought "You're such a loser."* You are not this thought; this thought isn't you. You still acknowledge that this thought is present and potentially painful. And you can also create a little space between you and this thought, so you don't get so hooked.

The less hooked you get, the more intentional you can be about how you want to engage with this thought, and how much you want to let it influence your behaviors. Whereas when you had this thought before, you believed it—and would RSVP no to that get-together invite because others might see you're a loser.

Now you notice the thought and any associated feelings. You figure out how to be with these feelings and decide that regardless of what your mind says, your value of friendship means that you will RSVP yes. And show up to this event the best way you can.

Regardless of whether the event goes horribly or beautifully, at least you know going to the event was in line with your friendship value.

Here's another small but powerful way to separate from thoughts that aren't serving you.

Exercise: Buying the Thought

1. Consider a situation where you're currently feeling stuck.

2. Now notice what thoughts your mind tries to persuade you to believe about this situation.
3. Imagine your mind is a persistent salesman who is highly motivated to sell you this thought. Are you buying what the salesman is saying? Are you buying that thought?
4. If yes, write down which thought you're buying into the most.
5. Now you're going to see where this thought leads you. When you buy into this thought, what happens to your behaviors? What are you more likely to do? What are you less likely to do? Write those down.
6. Pause and reflect: Are these behaviors moving you closer to the type of person you want to be—or further away?

If they're moving you away, you might want to reconsider buying this thought, no matter how hard the salesman tries to convince you.

I'm hoping you're starting to see how this subtle but powerful shift in changing your relationship with thoughts can help you. The more you do this, the more you can step into living your life the way you want to and see what that feels like.

Chapter 13

Your Mind, Making Sense of Who You Are

It can be challenging to step back from your thoughts, because thoughts can make sense, explain things, and make up the story of who you are.

As you've read, your mind is an analytical machine; it likes having answers for why things happen and justifications to explain behaviors or situations. For instance, if you struggle with social anxiety, and I asked, "Why do you think you struggle with social anxiety?" you might respond, "Well, I was bullied throughout my life." That reason might make perfect sense. It might even sound like a reasonable explanation for your enduring struggle.

Ironically, the more you believe you have "good rationales" for something, the more you buy into these stories. And the less likely you are to buy into thoughts that you can change, because you have a "good reason" for struggling with social anxiety.

I'm not trying to invalidate your experience here; it's your experience. I want you to recognize that holding onto this formula—*I was bullied; therefore I have social anxiety*—means you might not be leaving room for other possibilities. Maybe being bullied is one reason that you have social anxiety, or maybe not. If being bullied is not the cause of your social anxiety, perhaps you have more control over your behaviors, and greater ability to change them.

And the bullying is just one explanation. Your mind works by holding onto specific experiences in your life and adding an internal snapshot to the album of your life and who you are. But you give certain screenshots more weight than others because they make more sense or feel significant. For instance, if I asked what you did five weeks after your twenty-first birthday, can you recall? Did you take a mental screenshot to refer to?

You might be able to recall only if you did something memorable.

But if I asked, "What did you do on your twenty-first birthday?" you're likelier to have a mental screenshot of that day (a legal milestone in many societies) and hold onto the memory. It could either work for you or not, depending on how your mind made meaning of that event.

A comforting story could be:

> I went to a nightclub with friends and partied my newly legal butt off. I had a blast trying new drinks and showing off my ID. I felt connected to and valued by my friends. I entered adulthood surrounded by music, friends, and drinks; what more could I ask for?

When recalling the internal screenshot of that night, you think, *It was one of the best nights ever.* This reminds you of the importance of your friendships, and you dedicate time to fostering these types of relationships.

But let's say that day and story went differently:

> I planned a party and invited fifteen people. Only five people showed up! I felt like such a loser! I was so embarrassed. I felt so lonely and bummed. So I drank too much, got violently sick, and threw up in my friend's backseat. He was not happy with me.

Considering this internal image, you might promptly recall, *Everyone flaked. I'm such a nobody.* This memory influences you to avoid putting yourself out there in friendships, to prevent getting hurt again.

Exercise: Social Media Feed

Knowing which stories, events, or reasons impact your life can help you detach from them when they're not working for you. It's helpful to identify which mental screenshots serve as you as reasons why you are the way you are.

1. Imagine a social media feed you might find on Instagram or another platform.

2. In your notebook, list which events your mind has attached more meaning to. Fill this feed with mental screenshots of the events that make up who you are. Include both happy and painful ones. The only criterion is that your mind says these are the important ones. Fill in the feed with five to ten "posts" and write the associated captions for each. Come back when you're done.

3. Now consider how your mind boiled down your entire life into a handful of events. What about all the other moments? Are they somehow less significant? Identify which events serve as examples that your inner critic uses when reciting the reasons you're not enough. For instance, answer the question: *The reason I'm not worthy is:*

4. See if it's linked to any of the posts on your feed.

    How curious. Look at what your mind did there.

5. Continue identifying which posts fuel your negative self-talk—even homing in on one that seems the hardest to take in.

6. Spend a couple of minutes directing your attention to this post. Notice what happens to you. What does that feel like, to be so zoomed in on this one post?

7. Now slowly expand your attention and zoom out of this painful post as if your attention is a spotlight on a stage. Instead of illuminating just one actor, you're lighting up the entire set.
8. Zoom out to take in the entire feed, both the joyful and the painful posts. Also, notice the white space between the posts and remind yourself of all the small events missing in this feed.
9. What is it like to take in the entire feed? To acknowledge the ones missing?

To free up some breathing room from this painful post, recognize that this one post is not the be all and end all of who you are. You are much more and have many more experiences than this one event.

Why does this event get to hold so much power over your life?

Next time you notice your mind has become too wrapped up with specific thoughts, you can ask yourself, *Am I too zoomed in here? If so, let me zoom out and take in the entire feed.*

The inner critic is skilled at stealing your attention and making it focus on what it believes is essential, including any mental snapshot. The inner critic can replay events from the past or get you all worked up about the future. Either way, it can be surprisingly skilled at ensnaring your attention and directing it where it sees fit.

Before you know it, you've been transported somewhere—you're in a completely different time and place than your current here and now.

It can be so tempting to focus on the past or the future, and sometimes it is helpful. Let's say you recall a recent disagreement with your partner in which she was unhappy with how you handled it. You can review what you did or didn't do and see if you can do something different next time. If this motivates you to make changes to help your partner feel heard, then reviewing this past situation was helpful.

When the inner critic gets involved, it can look quite different. Instead of becoming an exercise in understanding or taking accountability, it can trigger feelings of inadequacy, and you become defensive. Or you victimize yourself and take the "oh woe is me" position. Your partner then focuses on your needs, and you struggle to hear your partner's needs. In this instance, focusing too rigidly on the past is not serving you.

Let's say you focus on the future and consider all the possible *what ifs*. If you're considering a career change, engaging in helpful planning to prepare yourself can be a good idea. It might encourage you to have enough savings in the bank, reach out to potential connections, and update your resume. In this example, focusing on the future has served you well.

Now let's say your negative self-talk adds a running commentary throughout this process.

And once you've done all this helpful planning, it's just spiraling you into endless worry about all the things that could go wrong. It's convincing you that you don't have what it takes to handle it, especially if something completely unexpected happens.

It encourages you to obsessively review all the scenarios, even making an elaborate mind map of all possible variables. The more you think about it, the more variables your mind comes up with. It's trying to convince you to control your future as much as possible. This leaves little to no room for feelings of uncertainty. It might even convince you that certain things are in your control when they aren't. In this instance, being too absorbed by the future is no longer helping you. It's keeping you stuck and trying to convince you that you can avoid uncomfortable future feelings.

This next exercise is beneficial when you notice your mind has traveled in time, to either the past or the future.

Exercise: Dipping In and Out of the River (Harris 2021)

It's helpful to read through the instructions once, so you get the hang of it. You can also access a recorded version of this at http://www.newharbinger.com/52250.

Imagine that each time you're thinking about the past or worrying about the future, you've fallen into a river. Through some guided instructions, you will practice learning how to step out of the river.

You're going to start with something simpler to ease your way into this exercise. I want you to bring to mind something pleasant or fun to think about, whether that's something you're excited about, like the latest TV series, or a book, or a mental image of your latest enjoyable vacation. Set a timer for twenty seconds and really let your mind go to this lovely place.

When your timer rings, I want you to pause and notice where your mind is. Even say it aloud or write it down:

My mind is thinking about:

Okay, great. Now notice that you have two options here. One option is to dive right back into the river. The other is to remain out of the river. If you choose to remain out of the river, then take a moment to push your feet into the ground, really noticing your feet in the here and now, out of the river. Take a look around your environment and pick something that you might have previously overlooked. Even take a stretch if you can. And notice that you are here in this moment.

Great. Now you're going back into the river for another twenty seconds. Set your timer again. You're going to daydream about something pleasant again, following the same instructions.

Once the timer is up, notice that you again face two options. You can stay submerged in the river, or you can make the decision to get out of the river. If you decide to get out of the river, repeat the same instructions for a timed submersion.

Repeat this portion of the exercise about four more times, each time submerging yourself in charming thoughts or images.

Now that you've gotten the hang of this, you will take it up a notch. You're going to set your time for twenty seconds again, but this time you're going to pick a memory that your inner critic tends to bring to mind often. It could be a painful post on your feed. If your critic tends to use the potential doom and gloom of the future to keep you stuck, then identify one specific worry about the future. Excellent! Now that you've identified this, you're going to spend the twenty seconds allowing your mind and inner critic to go to town.

Once the timer stops, again be aware of your possible options. You can stay in the river or be intentional in stepping out of the river. If you decide to step out of the river, direct all your attention and focus to noticing your feet are on the ground.

Push each toe into the ground and feel your entire foot pressing into the ground. This time, take an extra second to scan your environment and describe one overlooked object. What color is? What shape is it? Stretch, and as you do, really notice what it feels like to have your muscles expanding and loosening.

Back to the river you go, setting your timer again for twenty seconds. Recall thoughts that your inner critic tends to weaponize against you.

When the time is up, notice that once again you have a choice: stay immersed in the river, or decide to step out. If you decide to get out of the river, repeat the same instructions. Spend some time reorienting yourself to the here and now, outside of the river.

You'll want to repeat this round of dipping into and out of the river with the painful thoughts about four more times.

What was that like for you? Did you notice by the sixth round, you started to become a bit better at deciding to step out of the river and being intentional about staying out of the river? Maybe your mind tried to keep pushing you back into the river. Notice that each time you become aware of this, it's another opportunity to practice being intentional about whether you stay in the river.

To get the most out of this exercise, practice once or twice a day to beef up this skill. Or anytime throughout your day, when you notice that you've been dunked in the river, take a moment to acknowledge that and decide to step out again by coming back to where your feet are currently landing, what your eyes can see, and how your body is moving.

Troubleshooting

In these last two chapters, you've learned how to separate from some sticky thoughts by not automatically believing all your thoughts and instead creating some wiggle room. Enough room to be intentional about whether you want to buy into a thought. You'll still get stuck sometimes, so let's review some common barriers that might show up.

Your mind will try to convince you that this new strategy is a bunch of crap and won't work. It will turn up the salesmanship to a whole new level. Or it might get extra mean or loud, so you return to the old ways when it was in control. The more you expect and notice this, the more you can sidestep it. Again, you're making next-level moves your mind is not used to. You've essentially pulled the rug from underneath it, and it's reacting. As we discussed in earlier chapters, your mind isn't just trying to be a jerk; it believes, in its deluded way, that it's protecting you and keeping you safe.

A straightforward way to react to your mind's objection is to start thanking your mind. Yes, you read that right. When your mind throws up qualms, say, *Thank you, mind, for that information.* The clincher is to not be sarcastic but genuinely lean into it—*Okay, my mind is doing its job and trying to help me here, even though it's going about it unhelpfully.*

You might also get stuck if you have unrealistic expectations when applying this skill. This doesn't mean that you will never get hooked by a thought, especially those oldies but goodies. Of course, you might have instances where you still get hooked to thoughts; that's common. You don't need to create space from *every* thought—don't make this process something obsessive that now you must be hyperfocused on. Sometimes it's not a big deal when you get hooked by thought. And even when it is, that's okay; once you realize it, have some grace for yourself that your human mind is still doing its usual thing. And you can decide to do something to help you create some space.

You might be saying you want to create space from your thoughts but secretly hope the inner critic will disappear. So you're still trying to apply the control agenda. That's natural, because, again, there might be a part of you that still buys into the perspective that you need to get rid of it to make changes in your life. It's normal to want to hold onto this perspective. Once you notice it, use whichever tool you prefer to separate from that persistent thought.

Another common trap is getting caught up by a thought because it is objectively true. You might think, *I can't change the truth; these are cold hard facts.*

For example, *I did cheat on that exam. For that, I deserve to be punished and constantly remind myself that I haven't earned my place.*

Whether true or not, walk that true thought back and see where it leads you. Would you rather (1) get so wrapped up in being right that you deserve to be punished because you cheated on an exam, or (2) decide to live a meaningful life starting right now?

If anything, this difficulty can highlight what matters to you based on your values of integrity and encourage you to do something different going forward.

As you learn to be more flexible with your thoughts, be mindful that any thought might be helpful in certain situations and not in others. You don't need to make a blank generalization that a specific thought is always faulty. Sometimes it really might work for you. For instance, if you're used to being someone that likes to do a post hoc analysis of a situation to see what worked and what didn't. Say you have the thought, *Oh man, I was too clingy with this new person.* This thought makes you aware of your behavior and encourages you to make helpful changes the next time. Then the thought might be working for you.

But in another situation, you've just broken up with someone. After your initial date with someone new, you do your typical analysis. But this same thought—*Oh man, I was too clingy with this new person*—leads you down a shame spiral. You question how you could be so needy. You might think, *I knew I wasn't ready to start dating again! This is proof!* Then you ghost this person to preserve your self-respect, even if they contact you to arrange another get-together.

The same exact thought does not work in this scenario. Consider the role played by the new variable (being newly dumped). In general, you can consider that each new situation has a unique set of factors.

Chapter 14

Opening to Your Experiences

Jessica's expression wavered when I asked her, "Are you willing to have these feelings of inadequacy when you speak to your boss?"

She's not alone in her hesitancy with the concept of willingness. Most clients express resistance and give me a look that says, *Are you kidding me?*

Yet by the time I've started to talk about acceptance (another word for willingness that I'll use interchangeably), most of my clients have acknowledged that the whole control system is rigged and what they're doing isn't working. They've started to drop the rope (remember the tug of war with your inner critic?) and are willing to hear me out.

Please do the same as I explain the process: being open to another way.

Your inner critic depends on your propensity to avoid pain, because it is a primary human drive. And specific internal experiences (feelings, thoughts, physical sensations, memories, and urges) are excruciating to sit with.

But as you've learned, avoidance has a cost, and persistent avoidance can wreak havoc in your life. Just look at your master list in chapter 6 as a reminder.

So, what's the opposite of avoidance? It's to do the dang thing! Whatever that thing is (we'll talk more about it in a later chapter). But before you act, you must come to terms with what is required internally to do the scary thing. To access the willingness to feel afraid and do it anyway, because it's worth it to you.

A prerequisite for confidence is courage. There's a widely held belief that confident people are naturally sure and have figured out how to not be scared. This leads to the notion that you, unlike those naturals, must learn to be confident to do scary things, but once you find the hack, your insecurity problems will disappear.

But for most individuals, there is no shortcut. When trying something new and unfamiliar, they either felt scared at first or still do. The difference is that they tap into their inner resource of courage and do the scary and brave act, knowing the fear will be right there.

Tapping into courage involves being open and willing to experience the full range of uncomfortable experiences when you decide to do something worthwhile. The same applies as you're learning to be your inner ally.

Up to this point, you might have needed help to do this. It's as if you've been fighting with a floating ball in a swimming pool. You don't want to have it and don't like it being there. So you try to push the ball under the water and out of sight as much as possible. But no matter what you do, the ball bounds back up to the surface. So you spend all your time and energy focusing on pushing the ball back under or holding it underwater.

But what happens? You eventually feel drained from all your efforts, and ironically, you've kept the ball close to you. If you let go of the struggle and allow the ball to float freely, it may get close and even touch you—or it may float away.

Notice what happens to you then: You've freed up your hands and feet, allowing you to enjoy swimming in the pool regardless of how close or far the ball is.

So how can you let go of struggling with the ball?

Here's one exercise that will get the ball rolling.

Exercise: Physicalizing Internal Experience (Zettle n.d.)

It's best to read through the exercise once before doing it. You can also access a recorded version in the free tools at http://www.newharbinger.com/52250.

Take a moment to get in a comfortable position, seated, standing, or lying down. If you can, close your eyes. If not, choose a spot before you to maintain a soft focus.

Tune in to your body. Observe where you can feel the breath most prominently. No need to change the pace of breathing; breath naturally. Notice where your body makes contact with anything. Describe what it feels like touching your body.

Now, consider one uncomfortable feeling (fear, sadness, anger, and the like) or a physical sensation (rapid heartbeat, chest tightness, and the like) that you struggle with. Something akin to that ball that you may try to push underneath the water.

Now imagine taking a crayon and outlining around your entire body.

Imagine grabbing that uncomfortable feeling or physical sensation and putting it about four or five feet in front of you. As you imagine this, answer the following questions. Pause to consider each one before moving to the next.

- If this feeling or physical sensation had a size, how big would it be?
- If it had a color, what color would it be?
- If it had a speed, how fast or slow would it go?
- If it had a shape, what would it be?
- If it had weight, how much would it weigh?

Now imagine being able to reach out and touch it.

- What temperature is it when you touch it?

- What type of texture does it have?

    Take one last look at this experience. Slowly bring it back into your body. Notice how intense this feeling or sensation feels. Slowly breathe into and out of that spot in your body where you feel this experience the most. Allowing it to be what it is—nothing more, nothing less.

    When you're ready, you can release your focus on the breath. Notice again what your body is making contact with. Open your eyes or let go of the soft focus. Slowly reorient yourself to the room by glancing around.

Repeat this exercise for any uncomfortable feeling and physical sensation that you tend to resist.

The more you practice making room for any internal experience that gets in your way, the more you can pursue the important things despite these experiences occurring.

Chapter 15

Is That a Shark?

Jessica was coming around to the idea of being open to a new relationship. But she was still struggling to put herself out there and start dating. She'd recently broken up with a guy who treated her poorly, but she doubted whether she could do better. She considered reuniting with him. At times that option seemed more manageable than needing to confront all the overwhelming thoughts and feelings of going on a first date again.

As we discussed her options, it became clear that her ex could not meet her needs. To have the potential to be in a fulfilling romantic relationship, she had to be willing to experience all types of uncomfortable experiences at different stages. Her current step was being ready to go on a first date again.

We identified what she'd have to make room for:
- Feeling the anxiety in her body when she even thought of a first date.
- Noticing the thoughts her inner critic hurls at her: *Oh, this could go so wrong. He might think you don't look anything like your profile pic. Plus, you don't have anything fun or*

interesting to say. He'll probably be counting the seconds until the date is over.
- Sitting with the knot in her stomach, her heart racing, and tightness in her chest.
- Experiencing the feeling of shame that makes her want to run and hide under the covers.
- Naming the thoughts that tell her, *You're too fat. Too boring. You'll never find anyone. Just go back to Adam. He's the best you can do!*
- Restraining the urge to cancel the date.

When you're thinking of tackling a new situation and feel overwhelmed, it's as if you're swimming in the ocean and suddenly spotted a shark. Your heart feels like it will leap out of your chest. You're trying to hightail it out of there, but you're just not fast enough. As your life flashes before your eyes, you think, *Dammit, I should have gone on that first date!* Thankfully, the closer it gets, the more you realize, Oh, wait—it's not a shark, but a school of fish. Each fish doesn't look so menacing or threatening.

Taking on a new experience can feel like you're about to be a shark's breakfast. But when you get curious, you see it's made of different tiny fish. Taken individually, these smaller fish feel much more manageable to swim with.

For this next exercise, you'll swim with one of your perceived sharks and identify all the tiny nonthreatening fish that make it up.

Exercise: School of Fish (Guarna 2007)

Take out your notebook and write down a difficult situation you're wrestling with. When you think about it, the shark appears.

Now imagine pausing long enough to get closer. You see something like this:

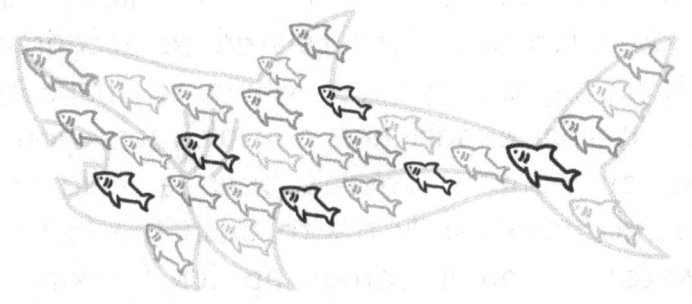

And each fish stands for something different. Some fish are thoughts, others are feelings, some are bodily sensations, and others stand for behavioral urges.

Thankfully, when you look at each fish by itself, it doesn't feel as intimidating. Make some quick notes about the fish in your school.

Now that you've identified each element, consider which is so bad and unbearable that you absolutely *cannot* have it. Which sensations *must go away right now*? Have you experienced each of these components before and survived to tell the tale?

Again, are you willing to make space for all these fishes when pursuing something that's meaningful to you?

Troubleshooting

I hope you're starting to get the gist—there is no workaround for having and accepting your internal experiences. But let's clarify some common misconceptions related to acceptance.

Declaring that you're willing to make room for an internal experience doesn't mean you have to like or want it. There's been a valid reason for you to desperately try to push the ball under the water. When it comes up, it's freaking hard to make room for it, and at times pushing it down has worked.

So don't confuse being willing with liking or wanting the internal experience, especially regarding your inner critic. The things it says hit deep in your soul. I don't pretend that you will like it.

I'm talking about the concept of befriending your internal experiences and adopting an open and curious stance—being able to lean into them, experience them, and even learn from them. Listen, sometimes that might happen! And eventually, over time, you might be able to befriend experiences more because you've gained practice in being open. Sometimes it will still be hard to befriend it, but at least you're willing to have that discomfort, because the cost of your struggle to submerge it isn't worth it. Simply being open to its presence might be enough at times.

Even the word "acceptance" can be tough to swallow because it can conjure images of "just giving in" or "losing." That's not what I'm referring to, either. If you get all hung up on the word, use any of the following instead: willingness, making room for, making space for, openness, or anything else that works as you adopt this stance toward your internal experiences.

Willingness isn't just white-knuckling it. White-knuckling is a more tense and strained approach, not the more flexible, open perspective we're aiming for. There's a different felt sense in the white-knuckled approach, almost like you're teetering on edge and any slight variation in the plan might knock you off. As if you're rigidly bearing it, jaw clenched, teeth gritted. In contrast, willingness takes a softer approach, such as *Okay, here's my experience. I'm going to allow it just to be.* Consciously trying to lose some of the tension around it. Which I know can be hard to muster, especially with some painful events.

There's another common fear: that by making room for painful experiences, you might open Pandora's box. And that once that box is open, there's no turning back. You'll be flooded with a range of painful and unmanageable experiences.

You might even be worse off and regress. This can be especially true if you've had a firm hold on avoidance up to this point. The prospect of experiencing any discomfort is like stepping into a whole new world.

Or, if you have a history of trauma, it can be common to fear making space for these experiences. You might even think, *You don't understand how painful this is for me. If you did, you wouldn't tell me to make room for it.* To be clear, in no way do I want you to get the message that my urging your willingness somehow means invalidating how raw your pain is. Your pain is real, valid, and excruciatingly hard to sit with.

But if what you've been doing up to this point has also been shrinking your life, or the cost is too high, I want you to know that you can slowly learn to take in these internal experiences while embracing the brave and scary act of living your worthwhile life.

For both of these, I encourage you to take it slow. Start gently fostering this skill by practicing with easier internal experiences or situations. Even when taking it slow, have some planned go-to tools in case it ever feels like too much. That could be returning to your present experience, grounding your feet, and reminding yourself you are safe in this moment. Or being able to seek support from a trusted loved one.

And, of course, if any of this feels too daunting to tackle on your own, I encourage you to consider seeking a mental health professional to be your ally as you build up your own inner ally.

When taking on these experiences, it's easy to forget why you are doing it. You might have lost sight of your values (which we'll be reviewing in a later chapter). Any time you decide to be open and act, it's crucial to link this behavior to something that matters to you (a value). This will illuminate the darkened path when you feel doubtful about taking the needed steps.

I don't want you to take on acts just for the sake of them. For instance, if you genuinely have no interest in starting your own business but you keep seeing all those posts touting the wonders of being self-employed, perhaps you've started questioning whether you're letting your fears hold you back from pursuing this. In such an instance, being willing to feel the range of experiences might not be worth it for you.

However, be aware that your mind can be skilled at convincing you that you don't care about something when deep down it *is* aligned with your values. In these instances, ask yourself: *If I did not have any fear or other uncomfortable internal experiences, would I want to pursue this action?* If you said yes, you might want to reevaluate whether possibly this act genuinely aligns with what matters to you, but your mind has tried to convince you otherwise. If the answer is no, that's fine too, and it might not be worth it for you to pursue this avenue.

Sometimes you might notice a tendency to take this acceptance stance into overdrive, willingly looking for painful experiences to lean into just for the sake of it. In those moments, again, I'd encourage you to consider what this brave act is in the service of. Is it to prove to your mind that you can do it? If so, then your mind has gotten the upper hand again.

This not a one-and-done process. You can't just check off *Okay, now I'm willing to have it all.* Rather, the goal is an ongoing attitude of openness, one you'll have to lean into continually. Acknowledging that it can still be tricky, even if you've practiced for a bit.

Last, a word of caution about having a secondary agenda with willingness. You might tell yourself: *Okay, I'm willing, I'm willing, I'm open!* when in truth you're desperately hoping that declaring your openness to an experience will make it disappear. In essence, you've turned willingness into another undercover avoidance strategy.

Chapter 16

Coming Back to the Now

Let me share a bit of my own process with you. As I sit down to continue writing, sometimes I struggle to get started. That's when I use the following tool to help me gain clarity.

I'm noticing:
- Feelings of anxiety and apprehension.
- The physical sensations of weight on my chest and tension in my shoulders.
- Thoughts of *How do I introduce this skill that's both centuries old and an ultra-modern buzzword? I'm not a mindfulness expert like Jon Kabat-Zinn or Sharon Salzberg! What if I get this wrong, or it just sounds trite and clichéd? Which angle do I take?*
- The urge to keep organizing and decluttering my desk or computer files (or anything else except starting this chapter). With more thoughts: *Once my space is decluttered, I'll be more focused and ready to write.*

This ability to notice, name, and be present with my experience is a core element of *mindfulness* (I'll also use the term "present moment" interchangeably).

You've probably heard this term, whether from popular meditation teachers, celebrities who have become self-proclaimed expert practitioners, or most mental health professionals. I'm one of the many encouraging mindfulness practices. But since this concept has exploded in popularity, it can also lead to some common hangups or misconceptions of what it is and isn't.

When I introduce the concept of mindfulness to my clients, I keep it as simple as possible: It means noticing your current experience, staying with it, and redirecting your attention to what matters.

So, for example, if you're playing with your kid and your anxiety tries to take over the show, you can notice and name what's happening to you. Acknowledge that your anxiety will not magically disappear, but you can allow it to sit next to you on the playmat. And actively redirect your attention to whatever you and your kid are doing, because that's more important to you than allowing anxiety to steal the show. This skill—being able to notice what's happening, reduce your resistance to it, and direct the spotlight of your attention—will be beneficial when you're having a hard time.

Not uncommonly, many of my clients who struggle with anxiety and their inner critic also struggle with being present in the good times; there's this looming dread of, *What if this goes away? I'd better not get used to this, because I know it won't last.* Mindfulness can also help you foster the ability to stay present when life is going well.

A more formal definition of mindfulness comes from Jon Kabat-Zinn, a well-known professor and meditation teacher: "the awareness that arises through paying attention in a particular way: on purpose, in the present moment, and nonjudgmentally" (2013).

Ideally, you want to tap into this skill when you notice your inner critic roaring and the associated feelings are getting you stuck. Being able to see what's happening and building your *now* muscle with less judgment can help you reduce the associated resistance to your experience.

You'll notice that this skill is also a component of many other tools in the book. Sometimes it's even a prerequisite for the other exercises. How can you create distance from your thoughts if you're unaware that you've been hooked? How can you be willing to have an experience if you're in the dark that you're resisting an experience? You'll see that the skills in later chapters also require an element of being present.

Let's start with the basics. I recommend beginning with small, straightforward breathing mindfulness exercises. Your breath is a constant in your life and readily available to use as a focus to help you bring yourself back to the moment.

For people who struggle with using their breathing as a focus or tool: No worries. I'll provide other ways to incorporate mindfulness activities, regardless of what's going on with your breathing.

Exercise: Simple Breathing Practice

Like the other guided exercises, it's helpful to read through this first or access the recording in the free tools at http://www.newharbinger.com/52250.

Start by getting settled. If you can, sit or stand up straight, trying not to be too rigid. Uncross your arms and either close your eyes or choose to have a soft focus on a spot in front of you. If you can't do any of this, that's fine too. Just focus on taking a moment to pause, whatever you're doing, and try the exercise in whatever way feels right to you.

Now direct your full attention to your breathing. There is no need to change your breath's pace or rhythm; allow yourself to breathe naturally.

Notice what it feels like to have your breath flow in and out of your nose or mouth.

Focus on the rising and falling of your breath in your chest.

Now direct your attention to the sensation of breathing in your belly. See what it feels like to have your belly expand and contract.

If you notice your mind getting distracted, whether by making a judgment about this exercise—*This is dumb, this is pointless*—or getting critical about how you're doing the exercise—*I'm not doing this right. I'm breathing wrong. I keep losing track of my breath*—or something else, that's okay. Minds are prone to thinking, planning, worrying, and judging.

Whenever you become aware that your attention has been diverted, gently bring your attention back to your breath, wherever you can feel it most prominently. You might have to do this multiple times through this exercise.

Stay with your breath for a little bit longer.

Now gently let go of the focus on your breathing. Open your eyes, if they were closed, or let go of the focus on the spot. Look around your environment to come back to it.

What was that like for you? How often do you take the time to tune in and fully be present with the experience of breathing? If you struggled because your attention was like "*Squirrel!*" or if breathing triggers uncomfortable experiences for you, that's okay; there are other exercises to help. I encourage my clients to use their breath in everyday life by simply pausing at any point during their day and tuning in to their breathing—doing a short version of the guided exercise.

This can be especially helpful when you notice you're starting to feel something uncomfortable. You can use this breathing exercise as a general internal check-in to see what's happening with you or to help ground you back in this moment.

Some clients find it helpful to tune in to their breathing to ground themselves before entering an important meeting or engaging in a stressful activity. Others like to take some deep breaths before they walk through the door after a long and stressful day at work. Others prefer to have it become a more scheduled part of their routine—say, setting aside three minutes when they wake up in the morning, after lunch, or before bed. Experiment and see what works best for you.

Next, I invite you to try out an informal practice of mindfulness. This means taking any activity or moment in your day and turning it into a moment of present-moment awareness.

For instance, if you're washing the dishes, use that as your meditation practice. Imagine you're an alien; this is your first time encountering this behavior on Earth. Your job is to report all the specifics of these strange human actions. Here you are, tasked with describing this experience of washing the dishes.

Notice what it feels like to have water running over your hands. What is the sensation like? Is the water cold, hot, or somewhere in between? Is the pressure of the stream of water intense or light?

What does it feel like to put soap on the sponge? What color is the soap? What does the sponge feel like in your hands?

What does it feel like to hold both the sponge and a dish? What type of motion do you have to do to clean off the food residue on the dish?

Remember, your job is to report back; you've never encountered these elements before.

Try this next time you wash the dishes or do any other household chore you typically do on autopilot. What's the point? you may ask. Well, this mundane task is part of your living experience, and the more you can lean into the daily moments, the less you'll feel like your life is passing by while your mind has you off somewhere else.

Becoming able to do this in these everyday moments will strengthen your ability to do so when you believe you genuinely need it—when your negative self-talk makes you spin out.

Consider these suggestions for incorporating informal practices:
- Before you check your phone for the first time in your day, take a moment to appreciate the wonder of your phone—taking in all the details, noticing what it feels like in your hands.

- When refilling your water bottle, notice the sensation of the bottle in your hands. Or take that moment to focus on your breathing.
- When showering, notice the sensation of soap on your body. Notice how your shampoo feels in your hair.
- When washing your hands, notice the sensation of water or pressure in your hands. What do your nails look like? Notice the different grooves, ridges, and lines in your hands.
- When putting on your shoes, notice the difference in how your feet feel, outside of shoes and then in them.
- When making your morning coffee or tea, take a moment to smell the coffee beans or tea as it's steeping. Notice the sensation of the mug in your hands. And truly savor your first sip. Describe what it tastes like in your mouth.
- On your commute to work, whether driving or on public transportation, imagine you're a tourist in your town for the first time. See if you can notice something you've overlooked or never noticed. Focus on taking in your surroundings with the excitement of a visitor being exposed to this route for the first time.
- When turning on your computer, notice what the keyboard feels like under your hands, on

each finger. What's the color and shape of this machine?

- When speaking to a loved one, give them your full attention. Take the time to hear what they are saying and look at them as they speak (rather than on your phone, TV, or other distraction)—gifting them with the present of your full attention.
- When powering down for the evening, take that first moment of sitting or lying down to do an informal body scan. See what it's like to be in this moment before you do anything else.

As you can see, the possibilities are endless. You can keep coming up with your own tried-and-true ones. Or you can have fun with it and see what new moments you can use to practice your awareness daily.

Chapter 17

But My Mind Doesn't Stay Quiet

Don't get discouraged if you have difficulty using breathing-focused exercises or some formal practices. In this chapter, you'll learn about other alternatives that can work for you.

One way to tap into any present-moment experience is by using your five senses. It's easy to get all wrapped up in your mind's content and lose focus on the rich, intricate world of living that is always available. When you can tap into any sense, it can help you return to the ever-present moment.

Exercise: Using Five Senses

Take a moment to pause.

Now observe five things you can see in your environment—even better if they're things you don't typically focus on. Maybe you've seen them a thousand times, but take a moment to describe these items to yourself. Notice the shapes, colors, textures, and so on.

Next, focus on four things you can touch—the clothes you're wearing, socks on your feet, watch on your wrist, and so on. Identify four sensations of touch that you feel right now in this moment. Again, truly see what they feel like, as if you were touching them for the first time.

Pick out three sounds around you. Describe the sounds. Are they loud? Soft? High-pitched? Low-pitched? Where are they coming from? Relish hearing three distinct sounds. Notice how you can also hone in on one sound at a time, or expand your awareness by attending to all three simultaneously.

Identify two scents you can smell right now. Is there a general scent in the air, or can you pick out the smell of shampoo in your hair? Describe these smells and stay with the experience of the scent. Is it a pleasant or unpleasant scent?

Now notice the taste currently in your mouth. Did you recently eat something? Is that taste still lingering in there? Or if you have a mint handy, put that in your mouth and truly savor. Notice the experience of tasting it, and describe it.

Now let go of the focus on any senses. Reorient yourself back to what you were doing.

A quick way to remember this exercise is:

Five things you can see

Four things you can *touch*

Three sounds you can *hear*

Two scents you can *smell*

One thing you can *taste*

This is a great exercise to return to this moment, especially when overwhelmed by what your mind is doing. Or any time you need a quick and efficient way to ground yourself in the present moment.

Next time the inner critic has stolen your attention, use this exercise to recenter. Since your senses are always available, you can do this anywhere or anytime. You can also adapt this exercise and make it your own using one sense you gravitate toward. Maybe it's easier for you to notice scents than sounds; focus on using scents to help you return to the present moment.

You can also intentionally use objects to make any sense stand out. For instance, have your favorite essential oil close to help you focus on the sensation of smell. Or put a sour candy in your mouth and spend a moment using the taste sensation, particularly the tartness or bitterness.

Outside of your senses, here's one more straightforward activity to practice on the go.

Exercise: Soles of the Feet

For a recording of this exercise, visit http://www.newharbinger.com/52250.

Sit up straight, feet on the floor, arms and legs uncrossed; close your eyes or maintain a soft focus in front of you. Get settled, noticing how you're naturally breathing.

Focus your full attention on your left foot. Notice what your left foot feels like on the floor or in your shoe. Identify any specific sensations that stand out. Notice the different points of contact with the floor. If it helps, push your left foot against the floor and see what that pressure feels like. Notice how the different parts of your left foot feel: the heel, the ball, and the top. Now focus on the toes. You can wiggle them and see what that feels like.

If you notice your mind gets distracted, that's okay—no need to judge it. Just gently bring your attention back.

Now redirect your attention to your right foot. Again, spend some time noticing any sensations. Notice how much space your right foot is taking up. Focus on different parts, making contact with the floor or your shoe. Push your foot into the floor and notice what that pressure feels like. Notice how different parts feel: the heel, the ball, and the top of the foot. Now focus on your toes. You can wiggle them and see what that feels like.

Widen your awareness and take in both of your feet simultaneously. Try not to focus only on one or the other but keep both in your attention. Notice that your feet are connected to the floor.

Push both into the floor and imagine yourself rooting into the floor, solid and stable. Remind yourself that, in this moment, you are balanced and steady with your feet rooted to the floor. If it helps, you can remind yourself that here you are.

Slowly let go of the focus on your feet. Take a moment to notice yourself breathing.

When you're ready, open your eyes, and take a stretch if you like.

If you struggle with breath-oriented exercises, focusing on your feet is a simple alternative to help anchor yourself.

Troubleshooting

As you dip your toes into mindfulness practices, it will help to dispel some common myths. The most common one that can deter you from practicing is "My mind has to go blank or quiet." You expect that when you engage in an exercise, your mind should easily become emptied and still. And when your mind inevitably remains full and busy and keeps pulling at your attention, you feel that you're failing miserably, or your mind is too restless to ever be mindful.

The reality is that everyone's mind tends to wander or lose focus. That's what minds do. Don't stress over it or believe you're doing it wrong. When you notice that your attention has wandered off, bring it back to the desired object of focus. You're slowly training this skill of redirecting.

A helpful analogy: Imagine you're training a puppy. Instead of being harsh with the puppy when it tries to do its business inside the house, you gently redirect it to go outside. And you keep doing this, consistently, until the puppy learns to go outside automatically. You need to treat your meandering attention in the same way. When you notice getting distracted, gently shift, just as you would redirect the adorable puppy.

This next myth is more from an ACT perspective: "I must be meditating wrong, because I can't relax when I meditate." When my clients are practicing mindfulness, I instruct them to let go of the desire to relax or feel better. That's not the point, at least not from my ACT therapeutic stance. I don't want them to start using mindfulness as a control or avoidance strategy.

Now, sometimes you might indeed feel better after engaging in any present-moment activity. Marvelous! Enjoy that moment of peace and calm. Just don't get deluded into believing this will always happen, or that peace, calm, or relaxation should be the goal of engaging in any mindfulness activity.

Yes, mindfulness can help ground and regulate your nervous system. There are proven benefits to regularly practicing. But be wary of making this a "magic practice" that helps you get rid of uncomfortable experiences.

One common myth is that when practicing mindfulness, you must always be in the world of direct experience (present in the moment) versus the world of language (where your mind is thinking away). Sometimes you *should* be in the world of language. For instance, you should tap into your problem-solving mind when doing your taxes; focus on planning, and consider the tax deductions. Returning to the world of direct experience might not serve you well because you don't focus on completing the tedious task. Tapping into your mind's natural abilities can be beneficial at times.

If doing your taxes is hiking up your anxiety and impacting your ability to complete them, then yes, turn to a preferred mindfulness activity. Use it to notice what's happening internally, recenter, then get back to the task.

Another myth is that you must spend twenty to thirty minutes meditating daily. Most people will respond, "I just don't have that type of time." This myth is a common barrier for people to start practicing mindfulness.

There are a couple of ways to resolve this. You can probably find the time if you think about where to carve out twenty minutes in your day. Whether reducing time scrolling on your phone or binge-watching the latest series. I challenge you to see this as a game of finding the time. Understanding that there will be a trade-off—hopefully, you'll find it worth it.

I'm also about advocating for doing what works. So, if twenty minutes sounds too long, start with five or even three minutes daily. Experiment with different methods: using the simple breathing meditation in chapter 16, one of the many meditation apps, or searching YouTube. The goal is to do what works for you and start with what's doable. If even that sounds like too much, lean on the informal practices and practice for three minutes daily. Once you get a good routine down, slowly build on that and then challenge yourself.

Some might feel that practicing meditation is participating in Eastern spiritual beliefs that might not fit their values. Though the historical origins of mindfulness are linked to some Eastern ideas, you may have noticed that none of the present-moment techniques here focus on spirituality. That's intentional, because you're engaging in these exercises to work with your attention—a capacity we all have. Ultimately, whatever belief system you do or don't subscribe to, mindfulness is still essential to cultivate.

Suppose you are of a particular faith that's an integral part of your life. It might be helpful to see that there's already an intrinsic element of mindfulness in your prayer practices, attending service, singing, or chanting.

Yet another misunderstanding is that practicing mindfulness should be easy and natural. This might relate to other myths about your mind going quiet or beliefs that you "should" relax. With so many advocating for mindfulness, it can give you the impression that it's easy. And when it isn't, you might be tempted to give up. But much like other practices that you seek to make habits in your life, it takes intentional energy to incorporate mindfulness into your life. It can be helpful to pick a specific day you practice, so it more easily becomes part of your routine. And persistence is key. When you fall off, notice that and get back to practicing.

Chapter 18

Treating Yourself Like a Loving Friend

Matt emphatically declared that he works better when someone is brutally honest and harsh and calls out his mistakes. No coddling needed. He also believed this worked for others too.

When we discussed this further, I encouraged him to identify helpful mentors who had truly changed his life. He described their approaches as honest and kind. They'd held him accountable without criticism, accepted and tolerated mistakes and failures, and cheered him on when he got discouraged.

He realized the disconnect between his actions and how his most respected mentors interacted with him.

Matt's experience isn't uncommon among folks with a loud inner critic. There is a sense that they *need* their inner critic to keep them accountable and moving forward. They've concluded that's the only response that works for them. They might view being kind to themselves as being babied, spoiled, and ineffective.

For all of these folks, the concept of self-compassion or treating yourself kindly tends to feel like blasphemy. They have worshiped at the altar of the inner critic, so they struggle to consider a different way. This makes sense, given how much airtime the inner critic has had in their life and the instances when it appeared to work.

In this chapter, be open to the possibility that there is another way of engaging with yourself: the inner ally. Think of Mr. Rogers's style of communication and empathy. That's the kind of relationship you can achieve with yourself.

According to self-compassion researcher and professor Kristin Neff (2011), self-compassion has three components:

- Self-kindness
- Common humanity
- Mindfulness

Self-kindness is, simply put, treating yourself with warmth and caring rather than being highly self-critical. How do you talk to yourself in moments of struggle? Are you kind to yourself? Or do you put yourself down?

I'm guessing that your inner critic tends to get on the loudspeakers when you've messed up. And your inner ally is nonexistent—if it even shows up to the dance.

Common humanity recognizes that you're not alone in your pain when you struggle. Being flawed and experiencing difficult moments is part of the human condition. If you can acknowledge and tap into this awareness when you're struggling, your experience can serve as a reminder of the intrinsic interconnectedness of humanity. You are not the only one that knows what it's like to feel like an outsider or less than others. You're not the only one that has experienced fear, grief, sadness, anger, and all the other painful feelings.

You're now familiar with the concept of mindfulness. Self-compassion is about recognizing when you're having a difficult time and being able to be present with it rather than avoid it or, conversely, engage in ways that escalate it. It's being able to drop into nonjudgmental awareness.

The easiest way to think about self-compassion is to ask yourself: *How do I treat a friend when they're having a hard time? Am I harsh and critical?* When you know they're struggling, do you tend to be more supportive and kinder to them? Can you offer yourself the same attitude?

If you're like Matt, who endorsed being more direct and blunt with others, consider whether this has benefited your relationships. Have you felt closer and more connected to the people you've been straightforward toward, or has that been ineffective? Maybe you've noticed your friends don't come to you as often as they once did for advice. Maybe you've even gotten into a disagreement with partners or loved ones about your critical or unsupportive stance. Consider:

Which form of behavior and relationship better serves your values?

Think briefly about your child, a relative, or a friend's kid. Imagine they're having a hard time in school. If they had a teacher who was harsh about their mistakes, it wouldn't be very motivating or kind. They might even feel shamed by the treatment. Now think about a teacher who's kind and supportive. This teacher is honest about what the child is doing wrong, but they take the time and effort to sit down with the kid to review the concepts and help them get it.

If you're scathing and belittling toward yourself, you're responding to yourself like the first teacher. And odds are you don't even question whether this is the best approach; it seems natural.

You can develop the ability to treat yourself as the second teacher treats their students. You can be your own inner ally. That doesn't mean you're weak or that you'll become lazy or ineffective. It might even motivate you to move forward during tough times. And it can teach you to live with a sense of resilience rather than stress or fear.

One way to incorporate more self-kindness is by embodying the different qualities of self-compassion, especially when you're having a hard time.

Let's say you've had a horrible fight with your partner and said some not-so-nice things to them.

When you're alone with your thoughts and feelings, your inner critic has honed in on how "You're a crappy partner"—and keeps replaying all the mean things you might have said. The more your inner critic does this, the more you want to crawl into a ball and disappear from the face of the planet. You feel like the worst partner in the world, and your inner critic keeps reminding you how much you suck.

In this moment of pain, you can tap into the power of self-compassion by first acknowledging that this is a moment of difficulty for you (mindfulness). You can say, *I'm having a hard time right now.*

It doesn't matter what circumstances led to this moment of pain, or whether your mind keeps telling you that you deserve this punishment. This comes from your inner critic, and in this rough moment you're tapping into your inner ally. Because you don't need to punish yourself to take accountability and own mistakes. You don't need to verbally beat yourself up to be a better partner next time or learn how to prevent this. And if anything, the inner critic and the associated shame might keep you stuck.

Once you've acknowledged this difficult time, remind yourself you're not alone (common humanity). When you're experiencing pain, your inner critic might try to highlight how alone you are or how no one is as horrible as you. They'll insist you're the only person on this island reserved for the scum of the world. Remind yourself you're not the only person who has experienced shame, said something unkind to their partner, or dealt with their inner critic. You can tell yourself, *Other people have sometimes dealt with this feeling and messed up with their partner. I'm not alone in my experiences.* Or, *Making mistakes reminds me that I'm part of a bigger community of humans who are also flawed.*

It might be tempting to skip this step, but this feeling of connection is often helpful during this challenging time. It helps to understand that we're all flawed and we all mess up sometimes. It reminds you that you're not alone (a feeling that can make you feel even worse).

The last step is to offer yourself some sincere kindness (self-kindness). Again, imagine that a close friend called and shared a similar situation; what would you say to this friend? Would you tell them that yes, they should put themselves in timeout forever, that they deserve to feel like a horrible human being? Or would you reassure them? "Yes, you messed up, and that's okay; it happens to us all. Go easy on yourself."

If you'd actually be nicer to your friend and can acknowledge they need some tenderness, don't you deserve the same loving response? You can take this a step further by placing one or both hands on your heart. Give yourself gentle warmth, and tell yourself what you most need to hear or receive in this moment. It can be something like *It's okay. I'm human. I messed up, and I'm not a horrible person.* Or it can be *Mistakes happen. I'm allowed to forgive myself.* Or even *I'm still worthy of love and acceptance even if I messed up.* Again, find the words that feel right to you.

This may seem a bit woo-woo for you, especially if this is your first time practicing being nicer to yourself during a difficult time. I encourage you to tailor your words to whatever works for you. And if you don't feel comfortable touching your heart, that's fine too. Find what works for you.

It's more important to embody an attitude or spirit of self-kindness to yourself as you change your relationship with your inner critic. This means even starting to treat your inner critic and all it encompasses with openness, acceptance, and goodwill. Part of being able to drop the rope is seeing your inner critic in a new light. The more you are able to feel this benevolence toward your inner critic, the less power and control it will have in your life.

You can bring this attitude of compassion to any other skills in this book. When you're working on distancing from thoughts, you can be kind to yourself if you struggle or keep buying in to the content of your thoughts. When you're trying to open up to a painful experience you've resisted for a long time, you can be gentle with yourself throughout that process. When you decide to make values-based decisions but it doesn't go as planned, again, that's a great time to contact your inner ally.

Chapter 19

Wait—Who's Noticing?

Up to now, you've explored the pervasive role of your inner critic. Sometimes it's felt nearly impossible to separate who you are from all the negative thoughts your inner critic offers. And you understand that the issue is how much faith you put into everything the critic says about you and how that puts you in a jam.

One common way you can get trapped is when you hold on too tightly to all your different identities, personality traits, roles, and past experiences. Consider your responses if someone asks, "Tell me about yourself." You might answer something like:

- I'm a mother/father/parent of
- I'm wife/husband/partner to
- I'm a daughter/son/child of
- I'm a sister/brother/sibling of
- I'm a [your job description]
- I love [your hobbies, interests, and passions]
- I'm [qualities of your personality that you value]
- I'm from [your nationality or heritage]

It's common to answer that question by providing some or all of this information about yourself and having a coherent narrative of who you are. And to a certain degree, it's reinforced in our society through messages like "know thyself." I'm a proponent (and even support it by writing a self-help book). Still, this "know thyself" maxim can get you too entrenched in the roles and identities you hold on to—which can interfere with your ability to live a meaningful life. Even more than knowing thyself, I encourage you to *observe* thyself.

It's as if you've walked into a house with many rooms. There are all types of furniture and objects throughout the house. Some rooms are messier than others. The house's physical structure (the floorboards and framework) does not judge or evaluate all the objects it contains. It doesn't care if one room has many items or is bare, whether it's painted Barbie Pink or Eggshell. It just contains all of it without judging it.

Similarly to the house's structure, a part of you doesn't care what the inner critic says or makes you feel, or the memories it conjures up. This observing part of you is a stable sense of self that just watches it unfold. It doesn't evaluate your experiences, reasons, feelings, or sensations. This might sound a bit abstract, but stay with it.

The part of your mind that engages in problem-solving, judging, evaluating, comparison, planning, and reminiscing is called the *thinking self*. This is what you think of when you think of your mind. This thinking self also generates labels and identities about who you are. In the "Social

Media Feed" exercise in chapter 13, the thinking self would be all the posts and captions you put on the feed. In contrast, the observing self would be the feed holding all these posts. It doesn't care about *what's* being posted, the captions, or how many likes or comments any post has; its job is to hold it all.

How does this apply to the inner critic? When you learn to tap into this observer self more readily, you won't get so trapped by all the negative thoughts, the associated uncomfortable feelings, and the rigid evaluations about who you are, such as *I am worthless*. You can learn to flexibly become aware of the experience of having these judgments and be able to make room for them—neither buying into them nor endlessly wrestling with them to get them to go away. Your identities and rigid self-stories will become more pieces of furniture in your house. You then get to choose how you want to live your life according to your values, not based on what your thinking mind is saying.

For example, you started considering whether you should return to school. But you believe a part of your identity that says, *I'm not the school type*.

When you think about venturing outside the confines of this mandate, getting attached to this rule is not serving you. You've chosen obedience to this character—*not the school type*—over making a values-based decision. To be clear, I'm not saying you will decide to start school. I'm saying that this rigid rule could get you stuck without knowing what's ultimately driving your decisions (your values versus strict rules/role identification).

You can see the issue with this. In staying within the script of what you're *supposed to be*, you're sacrificing showing up to your life in a way that is important to you. Your inner critic knows this and banks on your strict compliance with these roles and identities.

Your observing self, on the other hand, takes no forms or identities. This core self can also serve as a safe space for you. Imagine that all the painful thoughts and feelings your inner critic generates are like clouds or storms in the sky. Sometimes they can get loud and bright, causing your dog to hide. Yet no matter how scary the weather gets, the sky is still vast and stable enough to hold it all. The atmosphere is still secure and unharmed in any way. Like your observing self, regardless of what painful content your inner critic stirs up, it remains unscathed and unhindered.

Another dimension of the observing self is that a part of you has witnessed your life unfolding. This means you can access different perspectives across time, place, and even people—the five-year-old self versus the fifty-year-old self, you as a principal versus you as a grandfather—and recognizing that you have a different perspective from someone else. Your view on parenting can be different from your partner's.

When you can access all these different perspectives, it boosts your flexibility and reduces your self-defeating actions. Tapping into this fluid self can also increase self-compassion for yourself and others, which is essential for your inner ally.

One way to grasp the nuances of the observer self is by engaging in the following exercise.

Exercise: Observing Self (Boone and Myler 2011)

For this exercise, have a sticky note or notecard available. You can also access a recording of this exercise at http://www.newharbinger.com/52250.

Identify one important area of your life. Consider who you are when you appear in this area as your best version when you feel pleased that you showed up this way. Imagine discussing these qualities with a close friend. Pick a few words that capture this and write them down on one side of the sticky note/notecard.

Now consider what gets in the way of showing up this way in this area of your life. Identify specific thoughts or feelings your inner critic brings up that serve as barriers. You can refer to your answer from chapter

5 if that helps. Select a few words that capture this barrier and write them on the other side of the sticky note/card. Keep it turned up on this side and in front of you.

Now make yourself comfortable. If you're sitting in a chair, sit up straight but not too stiff, uncross your arms and legs, and ground your feet on the floor. If on a cushion or floor, uncross your arms and sit up. Close your eyes or gaze at a spot before you, not the note.

Bring your awareness to this moment by taking a deep breath. Notice how the air feels in your nostrils as the breath flows in and out. Notice the rising and falling of your chest and belly. Shift your attention to your body and notice where it contacts the chair or cushion. Note the different sensations of touch and pressure there. Now shift your awareness to your feet. Again, notice the places where your feet contact your shoes, socks, or floor.

As you note the different sensations in your feet, take a moment to notice who's noticing. Acknowledge that there is a *you* that is different from this sensation. There is your feet making contact with the ground, and there is you noticing it. This is the observing self.

Refocus on your breathing. And watch this for a bit. Again, take a moment to notice who's noticing. There is a *you*, behind your eyes, watching this experience. There is the experience of breathing, and there's your observing self noting this.

Now consider the different roles you wear in your life: partner ... child ... parent ... sibling ... friend ... employee ... employer ... student ... With each different role, you might be a little different in each, yet it is still the same you in each of these roles. A *you* that stays the same no matter what changes.

Now, think back across your life ... and imagine the millions and millions of thoughts and feelings and other experiences you've had throughout your life. Sometimes sad ... sometimes happy ... sometimes scared ... sometimes ecstatic.

Imagine how much your body has changed since you were a child. Everything has changed, everything that has happened inside of you physically and mentally has been transient. But there is a part of you that is still the same. When you said "I" ten years ago, that was the same "I" you are talking about when you say "I" today. An "I" that is continuous. Stable. Secure. Unwavering. This is the observing self.

Okay, open your eyes and look at what you wrote on the note. Imagine the experience described on the note is actually in your hand; however, you make sense of it. Feel the weight of it in your hand. Then take a moment to notice who's noticing this. There is a *you* there, behind your eyes, who is watching this experience you hold in your hand. A *you* that is separate from this experience you are holding. This is the observing self. From this place, thoughts, feelings, memories, physical sensations—no matter how painful—cannot harm you. They are merely more experiences to observe and hold.

Sit with whatever experience you had with this activity. This concept is a bit hard for the thinking mind to grasp, because it can feel confusing. Yet that steadier part of yourself is still there. One way to access it daily is by asking yourself regularly, *And who is noticing that?* (Hayes 2020).

You can make it a part of your routine by setting reminders or picking a consistent time to ask yourself this question. Or you can use any object as a prompt. When you put on your shoes or open your front door, pause and ask yourself, *And who is noticing that?* Be careful not to get too heady in these moments. The hope is that you access the *I, here, nowness* of your transcendent self, even for a split second.

What if there's an inherent part of you that just *is*? When you get so attached to all these stories, evaluations, or traits, you lose sight of this other, more essential part: just being. That is enough. No matter what your inner critic says.

Accessing this other part of yourself can feel profound and have real-world benefits. Because as you've seen, when you want to act boldly, and your thinking mind is in control, it can get tricky.

Especially when holding on tightly to obsolete roles or identities can throw you into an existential crisis because you've put too much stock in these roles. For example, let's say you pride yourself on being a lawyer, but what happens when you retire, or if you can't practice again for some reason? What happens to you at that moment if you've held on too tightly to this identity?

Or change it to a specific role. Say you held on to the part of being a wife—but then, out of the blue, your partner decides to leave you. What happens if you've placed too much of your worth on being a wife?

Maybe you've placed too much stock in your financial success. But then you lose all your net worth overnight. What happens to who you are, then?

Chapter 20

Keep Raising Your Right Hand

It's possible to create some space from your identities and roles. But there's one important caveat: The thinking self is a master at explanations. It can be easy to miss the trap involved if that self generates excellent reasons why you can't do something.

One way to evade this trap is to notice when you believe all the reasons why. Let's do an exercise to strengthen your ability to do brave acts.

Exercise: I Can't Possibly (Stoddard and Afari 2014)

Identify a valued action you've been unable to take. Something that matters to you, but your inner critic keeps blocking your path.

Now identify why your inner critic says you can't do this, whether it's a specific self-story, role, or identity.

Okay, put the two together: "I can't possibly take [valued action] because I am [the reason why]."

Now you're going to do something weird for me, just for a second. Raise your right hand and keep it up until you're done repeating the following. Trust me, this exercise is more effective if you actually raise your hand.

Repeat aloud or to yourself: "I can't possibly raise my right hand. I am someone who is completely incapable of raising my right hand. I can't possibly keep my right hand in the air. If I have to keep my hand up for one more second, I might die."

Were you able to keep your hand raised despite what your mind was saying?

If so, that's great. This simple exercise serves as a reminder that you can do something with your hands and feet, regardless of what your inner critic says. You get to shine a light on why your thinking mind thinks you can't do something and still make an intentional decision to do what's important.

For example,

I can't possibly set a limit with my mother-in-law, because I am a good wife.

I can't possibly ask my coworker to hang out, because I am a loser.

I can't possibly build in time to take care of myself, because I am a selfless mother.

I can't possibly leave my job, because I am a coward.

I can't possibly have a healthy relationship, because I am codependent.

And still, raise your right hand! That is, understand what your mind is saying to you—and choose to take the valued action you wish to take.

Troubleshooting

As you practice noticing, it's normal to run into common pitfalls. One that stands out is just the effort to understand this concept of the observing self. It can be abstract and intangible to comprehend. Technically, that's precisely the point, because it undermines the thinking mind's agenda and programming. But since you're so accustomed to allowing the thinking mind to dominate, it's hard to comprehend this other part of the self.

This could be part of your experience, and it doesn't mean you're doing something wrong. It means that part of learning to tap into this other part of yourself is becoming comfortable with the confusion. Since it can be so counterintuitive, it can feel ambiguous. If you're experiencing this, that's fine. Continue practicing being open to whatever your experience is, and still casually ask yourself, *And who's noticing that right now?* If you notice the confusion, you are not the confusion itself. Again, I know that sounds like a Confucian maxim. But sit with it for a while. You'll likely find it'll make sense.

If you find specific explanations are more workable—such as thinking about this part of yourself as a container of all things, like the sky—remind yourself of that metaphor or any other that helps you access this skill. Or you can imagine that any experience is like an apple in a fruit bowl. The fruit bowl's job isn't to judge, avoid, reject, fix, or control the apple. The bowl works just like your observing self, simply making room and holding the apple, whether it's green or red, big or small, juicy or dry.

As you work with this sense of yourself—this ability to observe whatever arises in your mind, good and bad, and to separate it from who you "are" and what you do—you might find yourself better able to engage in another ability: perspective taking. Flexibly accessing someone else's perspective can increase your compassion, empathy, and understanding of others.

This can have valid implications for the inner critic—especially if you're more sensitive to feedback from others, which limits your ability to take others' perspectives. For instance, if your partner is upset with you, you might perceive their feelings as an attack on you and internalize it as shame and rejection. You might get too caught up with that inner experience and lose sight of understanding and expressing empathy toward your partner. But as you cultivate the ability to be an observer of what you experience, you may be better at putting yourself in their shoes, even in stressful moments. Now that you've learned to step back from your experience and immediate interpretations, you can open yourself up to behaving in ways that heal your relationship rather than hurting it.

When working on perspective taking, consider the different types of roles you embody in different places and how you might hold them loosely. Who are you at work versus at home? When you're on vacation versus presenting a project? This can be helpful if you believe you're persistent when it comes to your studies but have no discipline in health habits.

With perspective-taking skills, you understand that you hold ranges—you can be different people in different contexts. This knowledge can empower you to apply skills in one area to another. Translate some of your academic persistence to adding healthy habits.

When shifting time perspectives, you can access *you* from when you were fifteen or fast-forward and imagine yourself at eighty. Both can have tremendous benefits. Opening the door to perspectives and memories of when you were growing up can serve to increase your self-compassion and acceptance.

The term *inner child* refers to different child versions of you, including both nourishing and painful experiences. And the term *healing your inner child* refers to offering yourself

self-compassion and acceptance for what you experienced during difficult moments of your upbringing. When a situation triggers those same feelings as an adult, it might seem as if your inner child's wounds got activated.

Let's say you felt criticized by your father and believed you were "never enough;" now, when your partner expresses frustrations with you, it could trigger this inner child wound and this "never enough" feeling. Engaging in perspective-taking exercises such as imagining your nine-year-old self and then providing the warmth, nurturance, and gentle words that your nine-year-old self needed can change your relationship with this inner child. You might be able to increase your self-compassion and acceptance and release the hold that these feelings and thoughts have in your life. It can help you engage with your partner in the present rather than allow your inner child wounds to take over.

Similarly, tapping into imagined perspectives in the future, like the eighty-year-old you, can help you gain clarity. Shifting into these future selves can help you access your inner wisdom about what matters and use this information to make decisions.

If you struggle with more visualization-oriented exercises, this concept might be harder to follow. Because it's not relying on the tools of logic or your thinking mind, it requires you to access a different part of yourself. Again, that's okay. If you're open to giving it a go, make room for any barriers your thinking mind evokes.

It can be tough to loosen attachments to a specific role or identity, whether or not it's one you're proud of. For example, your inner critic says, *You're too dramatic*, and because of that, *no one will ever stay with you*. If this belief has dictated your life, letting go of it can feel scary. Because if these thoughts don't have as much sway over you, it means you can make mighty changes in your life—and that can be a terrifying possibility.

Let's say you're attached to a positive identity, such as *I'm a great father*. But your kid is having a hard time, requiring you to take uncomfortable actions, such as setting appropriate limits or giving tough love. Each of these behaviors is aligned with another value, like parenting well, but the identity of *I'm a great father* gets in your way. Your mind says that great fathers don't do these things or would have prevented such situations from occurring in the first place. The ability to detach from your self-stories and inhabit a different kind of self can be helpful in these challenging moments.

In the next chapter, we'll dive deeper into valued actions and how to develop an inner compass to guide you in challenging moments like this one.

Chapter 21

Seeking Your Inner Compass

Jessica lit up as we navigated her values and what she wanted her life to stand for. She gained clarity on what truly mattered to her. That helped her make brave life decisions regardless of what her inner critic was saying. She understood that finding her inner ally included engaging in her life in meaningful ways.

I know that sounds easier said than done, yet each moment is an opportunity for you to show up to your life meaningfully. Of course that applies to those big moments like your wedding to the love of your life or when you become a father. But it also applies to all the mundane little moments in your life—including when your partner is cranky and you can choose to show up as a loving partner, or when your kid keeps interrupting you while you're working and you can choose to be a patient, understanding parent.

I'm not advocating for perfection (that's a losing battle), more for an acknowledgment that even when you mess up, you can choose how you handle it. The best thing about this focus on values is that there's always a new opportunity for you to show up purposefully.

Having a sense of your values is like having an inner compass that you can always consult when you're feeling lost and overwhelmed by what your inner critic says. When you're tossed about on the sea of all these crashing internal waves, you can pause and access your inner compass to gain a sense of direction. That doesn't mean the waves will calm down, but you gain a renewed sense of why you're willing to ride out the waves.

Your inner critic's harsh rhetoric doesn't just increase your self-doubt, insecurity, and feelings of shame; it can also make it hard even to weed out what's *really* important to you, leaving you paralyzed. But when you've clarified your values, your inner ally shows up with a compass and a map to help you regain confidence in what's important to you and navigate the experiences that come up along the way.

What exactly are values? According to the *Cambridge Dictionary* (2023), one definition is "the principles that help you to decide what is right and wrong, and how to act in various situations."

Your values are what you decide is significant and what you want your life to stand for. But it's not enough to identify a set of values; you must consider what specific qualities of these values are meaningful for you, then translate them into verbs that you can act out.

Jessica identified the value of connection, which she defined as building trusting relationships with others, offering support to others and receiving support from them, and having relationships that make her feel safe enough to be her quirky self, engage in activities that maintain these relationships, and seek opportunities to build new connections.

She could refer to this list of associated qualities and behaviors, then act out this specific value. Even when her inner critic crept in and tried to dissuade her (and sometimes it succeeded), she knew she could check this inner compass and decide whether she wanted to move in the direction of her value of connection.

When exploring your values—particularly with a value like excitement, which can also be considered a feeling—be careful not to fall back into your control agenda, believing you have more control over internal experience than you do. It's important to identify true values and actions—specific behaviors in line with those qualities—and to acknowledge that you don't have complete control over what feeling states those behaviors will bring on.

Staying with the value of excitement, you might focus on engaging in behaviors likely to fulfill this value, like traveling, and acknowledge that you might travel and not feel excited at all. That doesn't mean you're not fulfilling this value because you can't turn that feeling on. You're still engaging in valued actions.

Start here to help access your inner compass.

Exercise: Value Sorting (Miller et al. 2001)

Visit http://www.newharbinger.com/52250 to see the Values List.

You'll be sorting the values into three categories:
- Not important to me
- Important to me
- Very important to me

First, review the list and identify any that fall into the "not important to me" category.

Go back through the remaining values and denote which values are important to you and which are very important to you. The Values List also has blank spaces for writing in values that aren't listed.

After sorting your values, see which ones you identified as "very important to me" and distill them to your top five to seven values. I know this might not be easy; just do your best to identify your top values. Write these values on your Values List sheet.

Now define your top values in your own words, including what acting them out looks like, just as Jessica did with her value of connection.

After defining your top values, consider what it's like to see your top values so clearly written out. Does it feel like accessing your inner ally? Does your inner critic make some commentary too?

In the last step, rate how much you act out or live your values daily, on a scale from 0 through 10 with 0 being never and 10 being constantly. For example, Jessica identified that she was currently at a 5 in her value of connection since she had two close relationships. She noticed that she held back in these interactions because her inner critic told her she was "too much" and others would reject her. She had also stopped making new connections, and she seemed to always seek unavailable partners.

Consider your ratings. Are any lower than you'd like? Be mindful of your inner critic using this to knock you over the head. That would defeat the purpose. Knowing where there's room to grow is helpful; beating yourself up just makes you feel ashamed. If low scores have you thinking, *There's no point* or *You're too pathetic to make changes,* then your inner critic has retaken the reins.

Instead of listening to the inner critic, view these ratings through your inner ally's perspective. Imagine using a social media app with all those fun filters, and you've turned on the inner ally filter. Anytime the filter changes to the inner critic filter, purposefully switch it back to the inner ally filter.

You can always turn to your top values list for guidance and direction. Even if your list isn't available, or there's a specific decision you believe isn't related to your values, having your values in mind is still helpful. Simply ask yourself, *Is it a toward or an away move?*

Is what you're about to do likely to bring you closer to what you value, or will it drive you further away? Even if that choice means you will not feel "better" now, but will still feel stressed, anxious, or afraid? This question also focuses on *your* behaviors, not someone else's or the situation's outcome, because you can't control others or the outcome.

Ultimately, that's the path to eventually looking back on your life and feeling you lived it with a purpose. You'll judge your actions by your standards (values) and be satisfied that you showed up meaningfully, regardless of the outcome.

But don't reserve this question just for significant or worthy instances in your life; it's worthwhile asking it about all your choices. Use it to pivot in your daily life: deciding to apply for that promotion, asking for help, apologizing to your partner, or gently redirecting yourself from beating yourself up after a mistake.

Chapter 22

Calibrating Your Compass

Now that you're grasping your values, it's helpful to consider other factors affecting how well you can rely on them, especially if you're struggling with clarity in one or more areas of your life.

It can be easy to confuse goals and values, because they're related. Goals are specific and measurable. When you accomplish a goal, such as working toward your health value, you can check it off your list. Say you set a goal of drinking 80 ounces of water daily for three days straight. At some point you'll either hit the goal or not. But the value isn't something that you'll check off on the list. It is ongoing, and you'll keep setting and meeting new goals that fulfill your value of health.

Living according to your values is like striving to continue moving north on your internal compass. You don't reach north once and for all. You might reach a northbound destination (checking off that goal), but you can still keep moving north.

Also, it's best not to assess whether you're living a value-based life based on whether you've attained a desired outcome. It's essential to keep in mind that life can throw you unexpected curveballs, forcing you to pivot on any goal.

For instance, you had a goal of joining the military but were diagnosed with a medical condition that prevented this. So you can't meet that goal, but could you find other creative ways to move northbound based on the important values that inspired your goal of enlisting?

If you seek camaraderie, could you find another group to participate in? If you value structure, could you build a specific routine into your daily life? If you value patriotism, could you focus on other ways to support your country, such as working on legislation or voter awareness?

Of course, it's natural to grieve the loss of your originally envisioned career. Learning to be flexible involves making room for the feelings of loss when you can't meet your desired goals. But your inner critic can use this letdown to blame you, ruminate on what you did wrong, amplify the feelings of loss, and prevent you from moving forward. You're seeking to cultivate a balanced perspective instead.

Consider, too, that you're the only one that gets to choose which values are important to you. This can be both empowering and stressful, especially if part of your negative self-talk is related to fear of making mistakes or needing to be 100-percent certain. There are no right or wrong values; you can only choose what you want your life to stand for. There might be some values you intrinsically know are essential to your life and how exactly it looks to live them out. But you might feel stuck in terms of another domain or value because it goes against your family of origin's values or culture, or for other reasons.

You might keep trying to make *their* values fit into *your* life, but once you drown out this outside noise, you recognize that those values are not significant to you. If you're unsure, chew on these questions: If no one could see you acting out this value, would it still be important to you to do? (Stoddard and Afari 2014). Or if your inner critic made no commentary on this action or your ability to live it out, would you still want to engage in this activity?

If you've allowed your inner critic to convince you that you're not worthy of living a value-driven life, that can lead to you feeling a gaping absence where your values should and could be.

Your inner critic can also try to tempt you to wait until the right time to act on your values—say, when it feels "safer" or when you've reached a certain point to qualify as "worthy" enough to engage in your life in a meaningful way. The problem with this approach is that your inner critic keeps moving the goalposts. Before you know it, you might have wasted your most precious nonrenewable resource: time.

When you're dealing with this pressure to pick the correct value or getting stuck in "I don't know," try taking an attitude of curiosity and openness to trying on some values and associated behaviors to see if they resonate with you. Let's say you decide to try on the value of caring, and you list the following related qualities and behaviors:

> Being available to help others: *I will offer and ask friends/family if they need help with something and be willing to pitch in.*
>
> Make others feel cared for: *I will pick two weekly behaviors to show appreciation toward my partner/kids.*

Try engaging in these behaviors for one to two weeks and notice your reactions. How do you feel about the way you behaved in this domain? Did it feel enriching or not?

Use these findings to decide if that's something you want to continue. You might find that showing appreciation felt more in line with your values than offering to help. Or perhaps you need to go back to the drawing board completely. That's okay. Use these mini experiments to learn more about yourself, and be open to any outcome.

Troubleshooting

You can get tripped up by the difference between values and rules. Sometimes you find that what you considered a value is actually a rigid rule in disguise. Rules are strict mandates on how to live your life; they leave no room for flexibility or mistakes, and they're typically driven by fear. In contrast, values are based on what you consider significant in your life; they are driven by striving for something, more about getting the carrot than avoiding the stick.

Let's say you value being a loving mother, which includes being affectionate, emotionally present, reliable, and providing for your kid's needs. These parenting qualities are essential to you, and you strive to achieve them in most instances. Next week you have a work conference that is crucial to attend. Unfortunately, it lands on the day your kid graduates kindergarten.

You acknowledge that attending the graduation aligns with your values. Your inner critic keeps insisting that *you are a bad mother if you miss this event in your kid's life,* which keeps you feeling stuck and unworthy. Of course, ideally, you'd love to be able to do both, but sometimes life events don't line up the way we want.

You discuss the dilemma with your partner and decide that he can go to the graduation and Facetime you during a part of it. But you can't let go of the feeling you're breaking a rule. Your inner critic keeps reminding you what a terrible mother you are because not being there misaligns with your value of being a good mother.

Recall that values leave room for flexibility and aren't based on fear. This rule, however, *is* based on fear: that your absence will scar your kid for life. They're sure to be talking about this in therapy twenty years from now. But realistically, how likely is that? Your inner critic has cleverly tricked you with this "rule."

Of course, missing out on this event in your child's life will feel painful. But you can also acknowledge that attending the conference aligns with your career values. You can give yourself some self-kindness and decide that, in this instance, it makes more sense to go to the conference.

Throughout your life, you will face multiple dilemmas like this one, where two or more of your values are in a direct clash. And there will be times when you must sacrifice one area of your life to serve another.

It doesn't have to be so all-or-nothing; you can find creative ways to reconcile your differing values as best you can. In the same example, say you acknowledge that you will miss out on this event in your kid's life. You explain it to your kid, make room for any of their feelings, and plan to celebrate with them when you return. You still lean into acceptance that you and your kid could have some hurt feelings about it. The only way you would not have these painful feelings is if you didn't care about being the type of present parent you value.

That leads to another common pitfall regarding values: getting stuck when you experience painful feelings and being unwilling to make room for these feelings when acting out your values. Jessica realized that one way she prevented herself from feeling rejected was opting out of living her value of connection. When you're making brave decisions to live out your values, you must be willing to make space for the associated pain when life happens in all its complexity. Pain and values are two sides of the same coin.

For example, you get nervous in social situations and feel painfully awkward when you think others will notice how much of a dud you are. If you turn over that coin with your pain, your value of having intimate connections with others is evident. The only way you'd get rid of that pain is if you decided to throw away that coin in the garbage. But that means you must be willing to throw out the other side, with your value of friendships. Are you willing to throw away this value to prevent feeling the pain?

When you're mired in pain, it's helpful to turn the coin over and shine a light on which value is important to you. And remind yourself that this pain is signaling what is vital to you. A popular ACT question I ask my clients is, "Are you willing to make room for this pain in the service of your values?"

This is where it can be easy for your inner critic to stir up your fears and allow avoidance to take over. If you can acknowledge your inner critic's hold, you can work on the skills to help you participate in your life.

Another tricky barrier is when you convince yourself something isn't important to you to prevent having to face your fears. This might get confusing, and I'd encourage you to be honest with yourself. Consider: if fear wasn't playing a role, would you want to pursue that desired value?

Finally, another way fear can keep you stuck is when it prevents you from acknowledging if any of your values have changed. Rather than making difficult choices, you rigidly adhere to the initially chosen path. You choose blind obedience to what you "should" value rather than adapting—that is, changing behaviors, which we'll explore in the next chapter.

Chapter 23

Shining a Light

A fundamental component of ACT is making commitments to change behaviors. I want your life filled with moments of doing—not *thinking* of doing, but making conscious decisions to change how you engage in life. Because your inner ally isn't just about changing how you engage with your inner critic. No, your inner ally wants more than that for you.

Your inner ally wants you to partake in your life. And it will root for you when you're struggling by quietly giving you the strength you need to ground yourself when you feel shaken; by motivating you to get up when you've fallen, to sustain the blows that life throws at you, to hold your pain lightly and gently, and to keep showing up intentionally to your life.

Your inner critic has convinced you that *not* showing up to your life is safer. Or that you don't have the wherewithal to live a valued life. And you've seen the cost and pain of accepting what your inner critic tells you at face value. It is paramount to define what behaviors you want to change, then commit to start tackling them.

Before identifying your goals, it's helpful to understand what's currently driving your behaviors and the payoff of engaging in any specific behavior, mainly to be able to distinguish between short-term and long-term gains.

Let's see how this applies to Matt's life. He kept struggling with his career choice and feeling stuck.

Scenario: He was a manager in a friend's restaurant but wanted more. He initially took the job to pay his bills while considering his next career move. He had earned a degree in computer science, which he enjoyed. He wanted to pursue something in that field, but indecision kept him stuck, unable to take any steps forward.

Behavior: Deciding to stay at his current job.

Benefits: He could pay his bills, although he never had much extra. He sometimes enjoyed his job, since it allowed him to socialize with his peers. He was off the hook from having to make any scary career decisions. He did not have to put himself out there by interviewing for jobs better suited to his skill levels and desire. He could avoid or delay the uncomfortable thoughts and feelings that his inner critic threw his way.

Costs: He felt unfilled and wanted a more purposeful career. He didn't feel challenged, since this job was not tapping his desired skill sets. He did not enjoy the lack of work-life balance that the restaurant schedule created. He also felt he wasn't maximizing his financial potential, which affected his desired lifestyle.

When we dove further into his inner critic's role in this area of his life, he was able to identify the ways it hooked him:
- It attacked his competence: *You're just not good enough for the field.*
- It reminded him of past failures, like interviews when he wasn't called back.
- It convinced him that his current position was "good enough."
- It predicted that even if he did get a job in his field, he'd be fired again. He would then be unable to pay his bills and be forced to move back in with his parents. Even worse, others would know how much of a loser he was.

When his inner critic got on the loudspeaker, Matt tried to avoid these feelings:
- Anxiety and fear about what could go wrong
- Feelings of inadequacy, that he is such a loser, that if he tried something new, he would inevitably fail
- Frustration with himself for wasting all this time and lacking the confidence to move forward
- Resentment toward others who he believed didn't deserve their success or had it easy
- Sadness at his current life situation

Now it's your turn to shine a light on what influences your behaviors and what you gain and lose in engaging in them. As with Matt's example, illuminating the role of your inner critic will help you tap into your innate inner ally's skills.

Exercise: Shine a Light on Your Behaviors

Take out your notebook or visit the free tools at http://www.newharbinger.com/52250 for the worksheet.

Think about a current area where you feel stuck or unfilled. Write down as many details as you'd like.

Scenario: Identify the behaviors you're doing, just as Matt did with his behavior of staying at his current job.

Behaviors: List any short-term and long-term benefits and costs of engaging in this behavior. Be honest with yourself.

Benefits:

Costs:

Return to the scenario and describe how your inner critic impacts your behaviors.

The inner critic's role:

The thoughts you're getting trapped by:

The feelings you're trying to escape:

What are your reactions to seeing what's driving your behaviors and associated changes so clearly spelled out? Are the costs worth it to you? Or are you ready to do something different?

It helps to get curious about what influences your behaviors. If you don't have this exercise available, at any time you can pause and consider what's truly going on for you. And more importantly, are you willing to pay the costs?

Even if a behavior looks the same on the outside, the underlying intention can be completely different. And based on that intention, it can be either value-aligned or not.

For example, two people are running on the gym's treadmill. You might assume that both are engaging in value-aligned actions.

But if you could highlight what's driving their running behaviors, you'd see some stark differences. The value of health drives person A, who has a desire to be physically active with their kids and be around for their grandkids' lives for as long as possible. Person A is motivated by their values, and they still have room for flexibility. So if they miss a scheduled day, they don't beat themselves up, especially since they missed a day due to being at their kid's soccer practice. They recommit the following day. Or they decide to do a light jog around the soccer field, which still supports their health value.

Person B, however, is driven by an intense fear of gaining weight; they are working out to make up for eating certain foods in the past week. Person B also woke up feeling under the weather but still decided to push themself because of the nagging fear about their body. They struggle to have an open mind about working out, which can lead them to push their body beyond the helpful point. They've even missed out on other areas of their life due to being unwilling to miss a scheduled workout.

It's easy to judge your behavior superficially if you don't dig a little to see whether you are making a forward move or it's a cleverly disguised away move.

The point is, context and different factors always matter. Steer clear of all-or-nothing explanations for your behaviors or making broad generalizations that every time you do x, it's because of y. There can be so many factors impacting how you engage, and each can subtly shift what's influencing your behavior.

For example, you tell others (and yourself) that you're taking a social media detox to improve your self-care. And while that's one reason, another reason is that you're avoiding posting about your new project. Trying to get the word out on this new project is related to your value of being seen, but whenever you try to muster the courage to post about it, your inner critic pulls you back. In this instance, avoidance plays more of a role in your decision to do a detox than you might want to admit.

But when you take social media breaks because you've noticed you're obsessively checking your social media, engaging in unhelpful comparisons that negatively impact your mood, and getting too focused on your number of followers and likes, you're consciously deciding to take a break because you've recognized that the relationship you were developing with social media was not ideal.

Consider these different examples when you explore what's influencing your behaviors.

Chapter 24

Showing Up

In the previous chapters, you identified your top values and became your own Sherlock Holmes when inspecting your behaviors. You're better understanding the payoffs and costs. Now it's essential to translate your values into actionable goals.

When setting your goals, make sure they are attainable. For instance, you might need to tweak your goal if you want to read five books a month but barely get through twenty pages daily. Instead, focus on a more attainable and smaller goal—reading one three-hundred-page book in one month, which would mean committing to about ten pages daily.

By making your goals more workable, you're more likely to check them off and create more momentum to reach a bigger goal. A common pitfall is setting too-lofty goals, which can set you up for failure. Instead, check your ego at the door and use the science of behavioral change to make your goals realistic. You can convert your lofty goal into a long-term one and focus on achieving smaller short-term or medium-term goals instead.

Next, create your goals that are measurable and time specific. Instead of saying *I want to exercise more,* specify how much exercise you want to do. Are you going to measure it by daily steps taken? The number of minutes you worked out, or the number of yoga classes you took? Then by *when* do you want to achieve this goal? Here's an example: *I want to do three twentyminute fitness classes in one week.*

If you can't measure a goal, you'll have no way to gauge whether you're moving closer to it. And it's easy to get wishywashy when your goals are abstract. One caution: Remember that you can't account for all factors; some will be outside your control.

Say you aimed to hit a certain income level by a specific date. You set this goal before you knew that a pandemic would hit and your company would cut salaries for some time.

In cases like this, consider the following: Are there actionable items you still have control over to help move the needle in your desired direction? You might pivot and work on three projects impacting your bonus or apply for three higher-paying jobs.

Additionally, there's a benefit in focusing on the process and behaviors within your control versus getting too attached to a specific outcome. Picture a family with two little kids, driving to Disney World. One little boy keeps asking, "Are we there yet?" and bounces on his seat impatiently. He can't enjoy the new book he was looking forward to because he's too focused on getting to the destination. In contrast, his brother is excited and occasionally asks the same question. But he can also lean into the journey, notice all the new sights out the window, and enjoy his book. In this instance, his ability to be present with part of the process shapes his experience.

One way to embrace the process is to clearly link your goals to one or multiple values. When you set a goal that is irrelevant to your values, it can feel pointless. Whereas understanding why you're engaging in any one behavior can increase your motivation, particularly when delaying short-term payoffs for longer-term payoffs (i.e., exercising, eating healthier, meditating, etc.).

This next exercise will help you combine all the concepts and better understand what you want to change.

Exercise: Plan to Show Up

Visit http://www.newharbinger.com/52250 for a form that you can complete. Ideally, refer to all the costs you listed in the master list from chapter 6 and your top values from chapter 21.

Seeing the costs again can illuminate areas where you might want to change and are unwilling to pay the high price anymore. But equally important is to see your top values so you can tailor your goals to what's truly important to you (not what your inner critic says).

Here's an example of Matt's goals. (You'll find his completed form with the blank form in the free tools.)

Value: Being challenged

Goals:
- *Long-term:* Find a job in the computer technology field.
- *Medium-term:* Apply for three jobs a week.
- *Short-term:* Update his resume in one week.

Potential Barriers to Short-Term Goal:
- *Internal:* The thoughts that he's incompetent and that updating his resume is pointless and replaying past failures. The associated feelings of anxiety and worthlessness
- *External:* Lack of time to update his resume, due to his current work schedule

Inner Ally Tools:
- *Internal:* He'll practice the "Buying the Thought" exercise to understand the impact of getting sucked in by these thoughts. He will also listen to the "Physicalizing Internal Experience" recording to help open up to the difficult feelings of anxiety and worthlessness.
- *External:* He'll try to clear a two-hour block during his week. If he can't, he will commit

to taking a PTO day and focus on updating his resume.

Impact: Matt shortened his Wednesday morning workout and go to work later to find a two-hour block. He initially felt stuck, due to the usual harping of his inner critic. He noticed that he was starting to disengage and wanted to quit. He took a moment and was willing to practice the "Buying the Thought" exercise. He also took out his Plan to Show Up and reminded himself that he'd committed to being open to these barriers and still showing up.

It took more time than Matt anticipated to access his inner ally, so he didn't complete the task in his initially expected timeframe. This made him want to give up. We further explored this in session, and he agreed that his inner ally would make allowances, given the circumstances. He allocated another two-hour block the following week rather than using the reason *I didn't achieve my short-term goal; I'm such a failure* as a justification for giving up.

As you can see from Matt's example, once he identified his long-term goal of finding a new job, it was crucial to break this goal into smaller actionable goals. If he had just stopped there, he could have been blindsided by the barriers that could have prevented him from acting. When you list obstacles, you can set your problem-solving mind to work by acknowledging which specific inner ally tools you need to access to help you ride out the waves.

Notice how Matt did not hit his initial short-term goal perfectly, due to needing more time than he initially thought he'd need. In the past, that would have been enough to stop him from moving forward. But he recognized that his inner ally is intrinsically flexible and compassionate while holding him accountable for moving forward.

Now it's your turn to complete your Plan to Show Up, using the free tool at http://www.newharbinger.com/52250. I recommend starting with one or two values and goals rather than tackling all these changes simultaneously in different life areas, which can lead you to feel overwhelmed.

As you review your Plan to Show Up, make sure your immediate short-term goal appears doable and realistic, based on your current position within that domain. Find a balance between pushing yourself out of your comfort zone and going overboard. Keep an attitude of openness, flexibility, and curiosity as you commit to these actions.

Last, when you're taking these new steps and your inner critic tries to sidetrack you, ask yourself this fundamental question: *Am I willing to navigate these barriers in the service of what matters to me?*

If the answer is yes, then affirm the following willingness pledge:

I commit to engaging in [fill in the behavior] with the full and complete understanding that I am open and willing to make room for whatever I might experience. And I vow to solve any possible barriers that could arise, because this matters to me.

Troubleshooting

Let's address some common barriers you may encounter when you're practicing this skill of taking action. One common misconception when changing behaviors is that you must wait until you feel motivated to act. Instead, focus on moving through the lack of motivation and making intentional forward moves.

In that same vein, an unworkable thought is that you must wait to engage in any activity until you've hit a certain emotional level: *I will engage in career public speaking when I feel confident enough.* It's more helpful to understand that you can do a public speaking event while feeling nervous and experiencing self-doubt (even the most experienced public speakers feel nervous before giving a speech!). That's the only way to build the inner confidence you desire.

Another holdup is resistance to having uncomfortable emotions and difficult thoughts—the unwillingness to make space for your inner critic. Because you're so focused on avoiding the discomfort, you forgo living your life. Hence, I encourage you to reread and honestly lean into that willingness pledge you just took.

Sometimes, even if you say you're open to the discomfort, a part of you might still try to engage in subtle avoidance behaviors. You might still hold on to the belief that there must be some way to bypass the discomfort. To be clear, if there's something within your control to change that will reduce senseless pain, then you should explore those avenues. But when you've exhausted those options and are still uncomfortable, you must take a hefty dose of acceptance when changing habits.

Engaging in any task can feel insurmountable if you struggle to connect it to your values. If you continue to struggle with a desire to change, that could indicate that you must clarify your values.

In this scenario, be honest when identifying your values, and take some time to flesh them out more. Ensure that you haven't endorsed values that don't resonate with what matters to you. You can also engage in some perspective-taking exercises and time travel to your future self to envision what you want your life to stand for.

Being inflexible can also show up when you'd be better served by accepting that you can't accomplish a specific goal and would be better served by a different behavior (perhaps taking a day off from work because you're run down versus going in because you have an important meeting).

Last, there's another sneaky form of avoidance: focusing on growth in one domain at the expense of other values that are challenging for you. For example, you might be good at tackling career fears and being more assertive, but when it comes to romantic relationships, you notice it's harder to express your needs and set limits. When doing your plan to show up, you could still focus on change in your career domain, but you'll probably be stretching more if you focus on your relationship domain.

Chapter 25

Moving Forward

Now that you're seeing how to access your intrinsic inner ally (whose superpower is psychological flexibility), it's helpful to know what moving forward in all different areas of your life can look like.

Again, my hope for you is that you're not only learning all these new concepts but also making worthwhile changes in your life. If you complete all the exercises, notably the Plan to Show Up, you have a sense of what that process looks like. This chapter will brainstorm some ways to shift within each of these different domains.

Relationship with Self

Having negative self-talk is not a unique experience; it's part of being human. Yet the inner critic gains strength if you respond to it with an intense desire to either avoid it, please it, or bear it. Now you understand how these responses might have strengthened it.

The first significant shift when you start accessing your inner ally is responding flexibly when your inner critic appears. For instance, you didn't hit your goal of eating your preplanned healthier meal; you ordered out instead. Afterward, you hear the typically negative critiques: *You see, you'll never lose weight. You can't even commit to eating vegetables. You're such a pig.*

You feel the wind knocked out of you. And you notice these painful feelings and a strong desire to numb the pain by drinking two more glasses of wine. Instead of instinctively giving in to this urge, you pause to acknowledge what's happening.

You understand that this is just your inner critic doing its thing and trying to get you to change, even though it's completely backfiring. You consider which inner ally tools would be the most helpful: self-compassion, distancing from thoughts, or being open to the experience. And then decide to make a cup of tea rather than having any wine (since wine makes you feel groggy in the morning and isn't aligned with your values).

That's just one of many ways you can shift when you can remove the fear of the inner critic and embrace your inner ally. Recall that your inner ally isn't in a fight with your inner critic; it understands its role and purpose. Because of this, it can gently hold it like a butterfly.

Key Applications

Practice responding flexibly to your inner critic and all its components. The more you can embody changing your reactions to your inner critic, the more you will loosen its hold on your life.

You will also notice reduced costs associated with any dirty pain (in this example, you managed to avoid drinking two glasses of wine, waking up groggy, and feeling worse about yourself). Recall that being willing to experience the clean pain that comes with your inner critic is normal and natural; that's outside your control. But you can reduce your efforts to eliminate it, which further negatively impacts your life.

That might look like being more comfortable with making mistakes and taking risks, because your inner ally will always have your back. You can count on leaning into this resource, making the world less scary. Like a young child who can have fun and explore the playground knowing that if they fall, their parents will be there to pick them up and care for them. Sometimes the child might even look back to check if they're still there and watching before moving forward. Once you can establish that same type of relationship internally, you know you can explore the world and scrape your knees along the journey.

That means you can continue engaging in forward moves related to your goals regarding yourself, whether that's exercising, eating habits, self-care, or any other realm of personal development, rather than immediately giving up or beating yourself up when you confront an obstacle.

I hope that, with all you've learned here, you will trust yourself to make value-based decisions and be able to make your own decisions rather than excessively relying on reassurance from others or being steered by your inner critic. The more you can make your own decisions, the greater the confidence you'll build, because you will have a treasure trove of experiences to turn to when you feel shaky in the future. Instead of relying on your inner critic, you can remind yourself that you've accomplished difficult feats before and lived to tell the story (though maybe with some gnarly scars).

You can lean into more moments of self-appreciation and acknowledgment for yourself. Not in a sickeningly toxic-positivity way, but in a genuinely authentic loving relationship with yourself.

To get specific on what to focus on changing, look back at the costs you listed in chapter 7. That will give you a good starting point.

Relationship with Others

Connecting with others makes the world go round. As social animals, we are wired to seek out connections for our very survival—and so much more. That's why the feeling of loneliness is a harrowing psychological experience.

Engaging your inner ally can make a crucial difference in your relationships. Allowing your inner critic to dominate could have led to unfulfilling relationships. It helps to understand how your inner critic has served as the third wheel in your relationships. When applying the book's tools to your relationships, refer to your chapter 8 responses, where you listed the cost to your relationships.

You need to understand what tends to be your go-to move. Is your tendency to try to move toward, please, and pursue people who are emotionally unavailable? Or do you tend to avoid and withdraw when it comes to relationships? Or are you somewhere in the middle?

By now you know that context matters and can change depending on new experiences, particular individuals, recent life events, past hurts, and more.

Dig deep and understand the core fear influencing whether your relationships can reach the next level. See whether your inner critic uses this fear to convince you to protect yourself, usually in ways that hurt your relationships or life satisfaction.

Then assess what you tend to do when you start to feel scared in relationships. How do you make sense of that experience? Does the inner critic show up at any point to further confuse you? What are the stories you tell about yourself, others, and that relationship?

For example, Jessica sought more reassurance in her romantic relationships when she felt scared that she wasn't enough. If she perceived her partner as unaffectionate at times, she would assume he wasn't as interested in her or didn't care about her enough. Her inner critic would grab hold of that and start to taunt her: *Of course he doesn't care about you. What do you have to offer?* She would begin to get anxious in the relationship. Unfortunately, sometimes this tendency went into overdrive, and when this fear arose she struggled to self-regulate or engage in trusting behaviors.

When Jessica started to explore this pattern and understood the role that her inner critic was playing, she was able to increase the instances when she could unhook from those hurtful self-critical thoughts, accept that this fear indicated how meaningful this relationship was to her, and ground herself in those moments. She became more aware of when to reach out for support from her partner and when to engage in behaviors that showed her partner she trusted him.

Key Applications

You'll want to change your go-to moves when they are based on your inner critic's taking hold, and to strive to engage more in behaviors based on relationship values, not fear. Yes, that includes being with uncomfortable feelings without automatically letting them dictate your behaviors.

The more you can do that, the more you can reduce your tendency to anxiously pursue unrewarding relationships—or inversely, you can limit your urge to avoid relationships altogether. That means less pushing people away or withdrawing when you get scared.

The more you can be in relationships the way you want, the more you might continue stretching. That could mean expressing your feelings toward others, understanding that rejection is possible (knowing your inner ally will be with you every step of the way). Or it could mean setting healthy limits in relationships, speaking up about your needs, and accepting the risk that someone might abandon you.

Furthermore, you can stop reacting when your partner gives you feedback. Rather than shutting down or lashing out, you can navigate your internal turmoil and be open to hearing what your partner is trying to communicate—indeed, you can stay curious to listen to the need underlying the complaint.

You might notice your inner critic trying to claw through, yet you can breathe into the places where it hurts and engage your inner ally to help you become the type of partner you want to be. Being in relationships includes receiving feedback and understanding that can improve the relationship.

I'm making assumptions that you're in a healthy relationship. If I'm wrong, I hope your work through this book has allowed you to identify unhealthy relationships or ones that no longer serve you. To be clear, this isn't to say that if there are any issues in your relationship, that means it's automatically wrong for you, either. Now that you've taken control of the steering wheel, you can evaluate your relationships, consciously choose how you engage in them, seeing how your partner responds—taking all of it as data to help you behave in the ways that will serve you and the people in your life.

Relationship with Achievements

To jog your memory, I'm grouping the domains of career, education, altruistic endeavors, and hobbies you want to pursue into the broad category of "achievements." In deciding what to change in this domain, go back to the costs you listed in different types of achievements in chapter 9. As you review the list, see if you notice a stirring to revisit any other achievement-related activities.

For instance, you may have had a goal of being a physical therapist, but life took you down a completely different path. Are there still ways in your current life to meet what gave rise to that goal?

Some potential changes include reducing the urge to settle when it comes to your endeavors due to fear—whether fear of failure or anything else your inner critic warns of. Remember Matt, who pursued his long-desired career goal? I encourage you to similarly clarify your values in this achievements domain. Even if you don't plan to change your current job, you might find the qualities you want in a career in other outside ventures. You don't need one job to meet all your needs.

Fear of failing and of being seen as a failure can be a giant trap that your inner critic might have used to keep you in line. You understand that experiencing a setback comes with pain, but you might now be willing to take on that challenge, since it's important to you. Ultimately, calling on your inner ally will afford you the risk tolerance to pursue endeavors that have an innate element of uncertainty. You will have a newfound confidence in your ability to handle barriers, or even failure, if it comes to that.

If you tend to overwork to drown out your inner critic, you will finally be able to release its hold on your behaviors and decide whether you want or need to keep up this frantic pace. Perhaps you'll decide that this need to be in overdrive is driven not by your values but by fear.

You might also be able to view your burnout or perfectionism with a new lens and understand that the same tools you've been applying throughout this book can be generalized to this other concern, recognizing the interplay between your inner critic and your overperforming behavior.

Since you're setting goals based on your values—rather than on rules, fear, or avoidance—you might notice you can let go of some of the focus on the outcome and instead be present throughout the process. Of course, you still have desires and expectations—and your inner ally is intrinsically attuned to being present, more concerned about helping you do what you value than about achieving a particular result.

Conclusion

As you wrap up this book, I'm hoping that when you still have these thoughts:

You're so stupid.
You're such a loser.
No one will ever love you.
You're just too much—no one will ever put up with you.

and any other negative thoughts, you can accept that your mind's doing its thing; notably, your inner critic is trying to catch your attention. Yes, it will still feel like "Ouch!" But the difference is that you won't waste your time and energy trying to eliminate or control these experiences.

You'll be able to make an intentional next move, embodying your inner ally's ability for psychological flexibility and making strides toward living a meaningful life. As I've noted, don't expect all these shifts to happen overnight. Most likely you've been engaging in these patterns and habits for a long time and they've been reinforced repeatedly.

Now for some final troubleshooting as you make changes and embrace your inner alley.

Troubleshooting

You might default to avoidance mode without realizing it, especially when painful experiences hit you at the core of your values. Remember that it's natural to want to avoid pain. And when you spot what's going on, you have an opportunity to pause and ask yourself if the efforts you're engaging in to escape this pain have their costs.

Maybe they don't, in which case perhaps there is no tradeoff here.

But if you're honest with yourself and realize there *is* a cost, consider whether it's one you're willing to pay. If not, consciously shift back to acceptance mode, accessing any tools needed to help you.

This can be particularly relevant when you get hurt or rejected, or experience failure. Your inner critic might use that situation to remind you to go back to playing it safe. Of course, these moments still suck and hurt like hell. Just remember that this is a trade-off of making courageous moves in your life. It wouldn't require courage if it weren't scary. And there must have been a significant value for you to give it a go.

That can lead to another hangup: losing sight of your values as your guiding light. Life can get busy, and your inner critic can get noisy again. In those moments, you might drop your compass and heedlessly engage in behaviors based on rules or fears. The minute you realize this, that's a fantastic chance to decide whether you want to go down that path or pivot.

Remember that at any moment you can access your inner ally and recommit to a value-aligned behavior. You don't need to wait until you hit a specific milestone or a perfect time, even if you've reverted to getting snared by your inner critic.

I also want you to have realistic expectations, which means you will get hooked by your inner critic sometimes. You're only human. Don't get too fazed by this. Learn what you need from the experience, and keep it moving. Don't do yourself the disservice of allowing these setbacks to further box you in.

Last, there is no way to protect yourself from feeling pain when life is unpredictable and you're dealt a hand you weren't expecting. Keep in mind that you're not alone in those moments but connected to a vast network of people who have also experienced pain. Whether you access your inner ally or your support network (or both) to help you in those moments, give yourself some grace, and appreciate the resilience you've gained by using the tools learned here.

I hope this book has served as a guide for you to let go of the struggle with your inner critic, showed you how to find your inner ally, and encouraged you to continue taking challenging and meaningful steps so that the you of five, ten, and even twenty years from now will thank you.

No matter what your inner critic keeps repeating, I believe you're worthy of living that life.

Acknowledgments

It's impossible to name and thank all the individuals who motivated and encouraged me to write this book. I can't thank the mentors in my training, including professors, supervisors, and peers, enough. The generosity of countless contributors in the Association for Contextual Behavioral Science (ACBS) community has been inspiring. And thank you to the staff at New Harbinger who held my hand throughout this process, particularly Elizabeth Hollis Hansen and Vicraj Gill.

To my clients, whom I'm continually in awe of as I witness their courage in the therapy room: It's truly an honor to be with you on your journeys.

Last, I'm so grateful that my family and friends are my constant supporters, especially when my own inner critic gets loud. I feel lucky to have you all in my corner—particularly my partner, Cesar.

References

Boone, M., and C. Myler. 2011. "ACT for Depression and Anxiety Group—Cornell University Counseling and Psychological Services." Association for Contextual Behavioral Science. https://contextualscience.org/act_for_depression_and_anxiety_group_cornell_unive.

Brown, B. 2021. *Atlas of the Heart: Mapping Meaningful Connection and the Language of Human Experience.* New York: Random House.

Cambridge University Press & Assessment. 2023. "Values Definition." https://dictionary.cambridge.org/us/dictionary/english/values.

Guarna, J. 2007. "School of Fish." Association for Contextual Behavioral Science. https://contextualscience.org/school_of_fish.

Hanson, R. 2013. *Hardwiring Happiness: The New Brain Science of Contentment, Calm, and Confidence.* New York: Harmony.

Harris, R. 2021. "ACT for Disrupting Worrying, Rumination and Obsessing." Webinar. Psychwire, www.ImLearningACT.com.

Hayes, S.C. 2020. *A Liberated Mind: How to Pivot Toward What Matters.* London: Penguin.

Hayes, S.C., and S.X. Smith. 2005. *Get Out of Your Mind and Into Your Life: The New Acceptance and Commitment Therapy.* Oakland, CA: New Harbinger.

Kabat-Zinn, J. 2013. *Full Catastrophe Living: Using the Wisdom of Your Body and Mind to Face Stress, Pain, and Illness.* Revised ed. New York: Bantam.

LeJeune, J. 2016. "The Absence of Criticism Is Not the Same as the Presence of Warmth: Shame, Responsivity, and Adult Attachment." ACT with Compassion. https://www.actwithcompassion.com/absence_of_criticism_presence_of_warmth.

Miller, W.R., J. C'de Baca, D.B. Matthews, P.L. Wilbourne. 2001. "Personal Values Card Sort | Motivational Interviewing Network of Trainers (MINT)." University of Mexico. https://motivationalinterviewing.org/personal-values-card-sort.

Neff, K. 2011. *Self-Compassion: The Proven Power of Being Kind to Yourself.* New York: HarperCollins.

Reinert, M., D. Fritze, and T. Nguyen. 2021. "The State of Mental Health in America 2022." Alexandria, VA: Mental Health America. https://www.mhanational.org/research-reports/2022-state-mental-health-america-report.

Shaffer, D.R. 2005. *Social and Personality Development*. 5th ed. Boston: Cengage Learning.

Stoddard, J.A., and N. Afari. 2014. *The Big Book of ACT Metaphors: A Practitioner's Guide to Experiential Exercises and Metaphors in Acceptance and Commitment Therapy*. Oakland, CA: New Harbinger.

Wilson, K.G., and T. DuFrene. 2010. *Things Might Go Terribly, Horribly Wrong: A Guide to Life Liberated from Anxiety*. Oakland, CA: New Harbinger.

World Health Organization. 2022. "COVID-19 Pandemic Triggers 25% Increase in Prevalence of Anxiety and Depression Worldwide." https://www.who.int/news/item/02-03-2022-covid-19-pandemic-triggers-25-increase-in-prevalence-of-anxiety-and-depression-worldwide.

Zettle, R. n.d. "General Therapy Manual." Association for Contextual Behavioral Science.

https://contextualscience.org/general_therapy_manual.

Diana M. Garcia, MS, LMHC, is a licensed therapist in Florida, and founder and owner of the private practice, Nurturing Minds Counseling. In her practice, Garcia helps stressed-out people feel calm, confident, and kick-ass in their daily lives. Additionally, she works with couples who are struggling to communicate and seeking to rekindle their connection. Garcia has been working in the field since 2013 in various roles, including primary therapist at various treatment centers and, most recently, as director of counseling services at a local university. She is fortunate to be a Certified Daring Way Facilitator, and is a member of the Association for Contextual Behavioral Science.

Real change is possible

For more than forty-five years, New Harbinger has published proven-effective self-help books and pioneering workbooks to help readers of all ages and backgrounds improve mental health and well-being, and achieve lasting personal growth. In addition, our spirituality books offer profound guidance for deepening awareness and cultivating healing, self-discovery, and fulfillment.

Founded by psychologist Matthew McKay and Patrick Fanning, New Harbinger is proud to be an independent, employee-owned company. Our books reflect our core values of integrity, innovation, commitment, sustainability, compassion, and trust. Written by leaders in the field and recommended by therapists worldwide, New Harbinger books are practical, accessible, and provide real tools for real change.

MORE BOOKS from NEW HARBINGER PUBLICATIONS

THE NEGATIVE THOUGHTS WORKBOOK

CBT Skills to Overcome the Repetitive Worry, Shame, and Rumination That Drive Anxiety and Depression

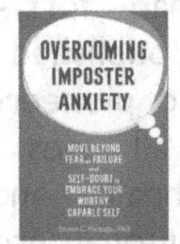

OVERCOMING IMPOSTER ANXIETY

Move Beyond Fear of Failure and Self-Doubt to Embrace Your Worthy, Capable Self

THE SELF-FORGIVENESS WORKBOOK

Mindfulness and Compassion Skills to Overcome Self-Blame and Find True Self-Acceptance

THE PAIN MANAGEMENT WORKBOOK

Powerful CBT and Mindfulness Skills to Take Control of Pain and Reclaim Your Life

ADULT CHILDREN OF EMOTIONALLY IMMATURE PARENTS

How to Heal from Distant, Rejecting, or Self-Involved Parents

LIVING UNTETHERED

Beyond the Human Predicament

newharbingerpublications
1-800-748-6273 / newharbinger.com

(VISA, MC, AMEX / prices subject to change without notice) Follow Us

Subscribe to our email list at **newharbinger.com/subscribe**

Did you know there are **free tools** you can download for this book?

Free tools are things like **worksheets, guided meditation exercises**, and **more** that will help you get the most out of your book.

You can download free tools for this book—whether you bought or borrowed it, in any format, from any source—from the New Harbinger website. All you need is a NewHarbinger.com account. Just use the URL provided in this book to view the free tools that are available for it. Then, click on the "download" button for the free tool you want, and follow the prompts that appear to log in to your NewHarbinger.com account and download the material.

You can also save the free tools for this book to your **Free Tools Library** so you can access them again anytime, just by logging in to your account! Just look for this button on the book's free tools page. ➔ **+ Save this to my free tools library**

If you need help accessing or downloading free tools, visit **newharbinger.com/faq** or contact us at customerservice@newharbinger.com.

Back Cover Material

Tell your inner critic to take a back seat

Negative self-talk can feel like an ever-present and very irritating roommate—one who gives you unsolicited opinions about your worth, appearance, personality, or life choices. But where does this annoying inner critic come from? And more importantly, how do you make it *go away?* Unfortunately, negative thoughts *will* happen from time to time. But you *can* change the way you respond to these thoughts, so they don't hijack your headspace.

This take-anywhere, use-anytime guide offers quick, simple skills to help you make peace with your irksome inner critic. You'll discover what drives negative thoughts, what you can learn from them, and how to put them in perspective so you can focus on what *really* matters in your life. You never know when negative thoughts will show up, crash your party, and crush your confidence. This book will help you to turn the volume down on negative chatter, so you can hear your *true* inner voice more clearly.

"For anyone feeling ensnared by negative self-talk and seeking meaningful, brave living, this book is a must-read."
—**Steven C. Hayes, PhD,** co-originator of acceptance and commitment therapy (ACT)

www.ingramcontent.com/pod-product-compliance
Lightning Source LLC
Chambersburg PA
CBHW011306150426
43191CB00016B/2351